CREATE
AUTOMATE
ACCELERATE

"A Radical New Blueprint To Building A Business
(And Life) That's Exciting, Has Purpose
And Gives You The Freedom You Want"
(prepare to think differently)

Leon Jay

Published by FHQ Publishing

FIRST EDITION 2015

1st ed.

ISBN-13: 978-1514701485

ISBN-10: 1514701480

Disclaimer:

All the information in this book is true and accurate to the author's knowledge. However he may be wrong. None of this information is meant, nor should be taken as, legal advice. The content is meant as inspiration and educational only. Any advice, suggestions or resources you should choose to use, you do so at your own risk. Every business is different and no results can ever be guaranteed. Please seek professional advice where appropriate. And most importantly, never let a disclaimer put you off from trying something new if it makes sense (so long as it is safe, legal and morally acceptable)…

For further information please contact:

Email: support@fusionhq.com

Web: www.CreateAutomateAccelerate.com

Cover design by Achana Tangsamritkul

I dedicate this book to all those who seek to create the most from life, who wish to give back to society, who want to find genuine happiness, and who wish to create true greatness for the world to benefit from.

ACKNOWLEDGMENTS

I would like to thank everyone who contributed to this book. It has been building up in me for a while, so I am grateful to each and every person who encouraged me to make this a reality.

As always, I thank the brilliant FusionHQ team, who keep things running optimally even while I am in my hermit mode. A special shout to Nae for the awesome graphics work (on the cover and throughout this book). Also to Sam Hudson for his help in highlighting the need for many of the chapters contained in this book. And, a big thanks for all the help in marketing FusionHQ, SendFish, and this book. I dedicate the chapter on gamophobia just to you. To Stephane Busso and Pitipong Guntawong, I could not do it without you guys. Tanya Hart, thanks for keeping our customers happy. And to the rest of the talented FusionHQ team, you are all amazing.

In the chapters that follow, I have quoted many great minds and some incredible books that have seeded the different ideas contained within this book. To each speaker, author, scientist, artist, philosopher, and entrepreneur referenced in these pages, and the many more that have helped me become who I am today, thank you.

A special shout to all the Coffee Monster customers that I have chatted with over the past two years and who have made me realize the need for this book. Mai, John, Mark, Emil, Zach, Lorna, Sebastian, Grant, Charlie, and many more—there is a little piece of all of you within these pages. I have enjoyed each conversation and debate that has challenged and clarified the ideas for this book.

Also, to my daughter, Aleshya Jay. You are an inspiration.

FORWARD

There is far too much written on making money and not enough written on how to do it for the right reasons.

This is a unique book that combines philosophy, science, and art to provide a guidebook to everyone who wishes to embark on the entrepreneur's journey.

It provides a solid framework from which to base your ideas, as well as strategic models for growing and expanding those ideas. It forces the reader to face the questions of what really matters in this life and how to make each day count.

Throughout my personal path to profit, I faced many challenges to my business and to my ethics. It was during those trying times that I wish I had had a book such as this to make those periods easier to overcome. If more people followed the advice that Leon gives within this book, the world would truly be a better place.

TABLE OF CONTENTS

PREFACE - A PERSONAL STORY WITH UNIVERSAL IMPLICATIONS

This is a book for anyone who does not want to compromise integrity, passion, and purpose for making a profit—yet does not want to compromise financial comfort for the sake of ideals either.

Let me explain…

I did not grow up in a wealthy family or around wealthy people. Nor did I grow up in a strongly entrepreneurial, or even a business-oriented, environment. I sabotaged my electronic engineering education (by refusing to take the final exam on principle of how the department was being run), which pretty much ended my prospects of a traditional career path.

I have been homeless and penniless and have experimented with far too many drugs for anyone's health. The few minimum wage jobs I have had included unloading trucks in a warehouse, being a care worker (where I had human feces thrown at me), and even working a six-month stint as a gravedigger. (Try telling people that at parties!)

You could say my life did not get off to a flying start.

During this period, I discovered meditation and personal development. It offered me a new way to see the world and a path for escaping the repetitive drug use, and it helped me realize that who I was did not define who I could become.

When I was twenty-two, during a year-long backpacking trip through Australia, I almost died while on a Vipassana meditation retreat (a ten-day silent meditation program). For two days, I meditated through an erupted appendix. By the time I was carried to the hospital, the doctors declared I should already be dead.

The strange part to this story is the fact that I knew I had appendicitis. And in my mind, I was fairly sure I was going to die. Yet I did nothing about it. The meditation course was being held in the Outback, with the nearest hospital, Darwin, a few hours away. I had accepted my fate, and I was at peace with it.

Surviving this experience changed the way I viewed and lived life.

Like many others who have been nose to nose with death, I developed a deeper understanding of the spiritual philosophies I had been studying. Insights such as "life is not about how much money you take to your grave," and "happiness does not come from how much you can accumulate" had always seemed like good concepts to live by. However, after having coffee with the grim reaper, they just got a whole lot more real.

I wish I could say that I figured everything out overnight, but that was not the case. For the next ten years, I went on a quest to learn how I could better make a difference in the lives of others. I studied naturopathy, therapeutic massage, and emotional release techniques. I learned hypnosis, NLP (neuro-linguistic programming), and other belief-conditioning methods. And I read every personal development book and attended every seminar I could find.

My interest in business started out from the necessity to make money (I was next to unemployable for any kind of real job). At first, it was simply a way to pay the bills. But then I became fascinated by it. I recognized that, used correctly, business held more potential than charity to change lives. It just depended on how this powerful tool was used.

(Businesses, when run well, are self-supporting, take care of their "volunteers" financially, and directly give back to the people who contribute toward them. Their contribution to society can be measured on many levels. If charities ran more like businesses, just giving their profits to fund their cause instead of giving them to shareholders, they would not rely on donations. Not that I am against charities, I just think businesses should think more like charities, and charities should think more like businesses. If run optimally, maybe there is no need to even differentiate between them.)

It excites me to see the new wave of entrepreneurs that is recognizing and embracing this shift in business thinking and ethics that goes far beyond paying lip service by being "socially responsible," The good of everyone involved, and indirectly affected, is finally taking priority over profit. There is now even a legal structure for acknowledging this shift (the B-corp, a corporation that can legally make society a bigger priority than shareholder profits).

However, I have also become saddened by the many lives I still see being lost through chasing money, without a thought to whether there is a better way to use the precious gift of time.

This book is about doing business and creating wealth. But it is not just about financial wealth. It is about making our lives, and the lives of others, richer on many levels. It is about living a life of meaning and value. And it is about how to achieve this in a very practical way.

I hope it plays a part in helping change the way you think, act, and experience your life for the better. If so, please pass on these ideas. Business by business, we will make the world a better place.

AN INTRODUCTION (TO GREATNESS)

"Nothing great has ever been achieved without enthusiasm."

– Ralph Waldo Emerson

D o you want to die having lived only a mediocre life?

Do you want to be remembered as being average at best?

Do you want to be remembered as having made a living by copying others and never contributing anything truly unique or special?

If you answered yes to any of these questions, you really are in the wrong place.

This book is for those who wish to live a truly fulfilling life. One that balances the need to make money with the desire to contribute and create greatness.

Let me clarify... I am not talking greatness in the sense of getting everything ego wants. This is not about becoming rich or famous. (Though it is possible for these to come as a side effect of achieving greatness, they are never the intention.) I am talking about a greatness that comes through making a positive difference in the lives of others.

I will begin by pointing out that Emerson never said, "Nothing great has ever been achieved without hunger for money, desperation, or aimlessly following fads." Yet it is often these things that are at the core of many new businesses and the lives of those who run them.

I won't lie to you. I can give you countless examples of people who did very well financially with this way of thinking. But many other fortunes were created in a much more interesting and meaningful way.

Greatness is not achieved through apathy. It is not achieved through focusing on your own needs or focusing on a series of financial milestones. Nor is it achieved by following the herd.

Being great requires you to be different. It requires purpose, contribution, passion, and enthusiasm. It is about creating change for the better. Perhaps a rough equation could be given like this:

Level of Positive Impact x Number of People Reached = Level of Greatness

Business gives us the chance to do just this.

The more people it can reach, and the more it creates a positive impact on those people's lives, then the greater the business is.

To be clear, I am not saying everyone should be the next Elon Musk, Mother Theresa, Bill Gates, or Ghandi (not a list you see together every day). We should not measure our lives in comparison to anyone else's. Only taking inspiration from them and working to improve ourselves. With a few rare exceptions, we are all capable of so much more than we realize.

Life really is short, being an average of only 4,000 weeks long. Given the fact you are reading this, I would guess you only have between 1,000 and 2,500 weeks left. Therefore, I encourage you to make each day count.

This book has been born from my frustrations about this very topic. I am frustrated with myself and how much time I have wasted. Perhaps worse is seeing how many others are doing the same, most of whom are chasing money instead of trying to achieve greatness.

It is worth noting that being famous is not the same as being great. But many well-known people are not great, and many unknown people are truly great. The same is true for wealth. Many wealthy people are not great (some are), and many poor people are great (others are not).

It is from countless hours of conversations with budding entrepreneurs that I began to realize that people want to achieve more. They want to contribute. They aspire to be great. And really this should be no surprise.

A while back Anthony Robbins identified what he called "the six human needs." These needs are in all of us to varying degrees. They are what make for a fulfilling life or, ironically, destroy it. Before I explain the paradox, take a look at what these needs are:

1. **Certainty:** assurance you can avoid pain and gain pleasure

2. **Uncertainty/Variety:** the need for the unknown, change, new stimuli

3. **Significance:** feeling unique, important, special, or needed

4. **Connection/Love:** a strong feeling of closeness or union with someone or something

5. **Growth:** an expansion of capacity, capability, or understanding

6. **Contribution:** a sense of service and focus on helping, giving to, and supporting others

Through his work as a business and life coach, Anthony recognized that people would do almost anything to get these needs met. In many cases, the methods they would use would be counterproductive.

During his TED talk on this topic, Anthony explains how a gangster pulling a gun on someone will meet the first four of these needs. When he pulls the gun, he is very certain that he will get a response. He is uncertain what may happen; anything may go down at this point.

To the other person at the end of the barrel, he just became the most significant person for a short period of time. And the gangster just established a strong connection between himself and the person he is pulling the gun on. It may be a connection based in fear, but it a connection nonetheless.

Anthony says that this negative example does not allow for growth or contribution. But, actually, I think it does. Even in a gang, there is the promise of rising through the ranks, becoming more skilled, and being given more responsibility. There is also the call to contribute to your gang and help support the other members.

Either way, we can see that this is not the most productive way to meet all these needs. Each is only being met in quite a superficial or transitory fashion.

Building a great business, however, allows us to meet all of these needs in a very profound and positive way.

Once you have built a sustainable business, you can reach a point of financial certainty for your future. You can also create routines that will allow you to predict many of the things you will do each day.

With business, though, there is always a sense of uncertainty, too. Meeting new people, creating new products, and facing ever-changing markets.

As the founder of a business, you will always be significant to your team and to your customers. By becoming a great leader, your need for significance will be met in a very constructive way. If you are only in it for the money, then you may end up being significant, but for all the wrong reasons.

As I have built my business, I have created many deep and meaningful relationships. The journey through life is not always a walk in the park. By supporting those who work for you, and who do business with you, you will build a network that will also support you during trying times.

In my experience, business is the most intense personal growth workshop you will ever attend. Growth is almost a must. Of course, if your intent is to create greatness, then you will be forced to grow more than if you are simply focusing on paying your bills.

The sixth and final need, contribution, should be the very foundation of business itself. You will contribute to the lives of your team and your customers. Of course, the greater your business, the greater your contribution.

It was for these reasons I tried to map out a better way. A clear path to helping people achieve their six basic needs, and their financial goals, without compromise. Indeed, I believe that, when these needs are in alignment, it becomes easier, not harder, to make money.

Another important insight I learned from Anthony Robbins's work was the importance of asking better quality questions. I can't begin to explain how fundamental that concept has been in shaping my life and, in particular, the contents of this book.

If there is one thing I would encourage you to learn, it is how to identify when you are asking a bad question and how to reframe it so you get more productive answers. As Dubner and Levitt, authors of *Think Like A Freak*, say, "If you ask the wrong question, you are almost guaranteed to get the wrong answer."This book won't try to repeat the amazing content that Anthony has put together over the years. What it will do is offer a framework to follow that will help you on the right path.

This book is broken down into three sections: Create, Automate, and Accelerate.

These divisions are really to provide the overview of the stages a business will go through. In real life, though, they are not quite so clean cut. Not only do they apply to the big picture, but they also apply to each micro-section of building your business.

There are many people trying to teach you that they have all the answers and that their methods are suitable for everyone. This is rarely the case. But how do you know what is right and what is not?

This book will teach you how to think like those who have successfully created greatness. It will also help you develop enough clarity to know when advice is relevant and useful to you and when it is not.

You will learn which questions you should be asking and, equally important, the order in which to ask them. You will learn powerful, but simple, models and frameworks with which to structure, automate, and then grow your business. You will learn to create something truly great...

Free Bonuses Worth $500

Including Additional Training, Resources, Landing Page Builder And Autoresponder

 Video training program to help further expand on the ideas in this book. Also includes a 28 day step by step program to build a list to kick start your business.

 Many resources you will need or find useful. Many of these are the same resources you would usually need to pay for, such as graphics and templates.

 Free landing page builder and autoresponder. This is all the software you will ever need to build, manage and mail your lists. A critical part of any business.

 Additional worksheets, links and updates as well as updates on any additional live training or webinars as they become available. Always stay up-to-date.

GO GET YOUR FREE ACCESS NOW...

www.CreateAutomateAccelerate.com/resources

SECTION 1: CREATE

"The best way to predict the future is to create it."

- Peter Drucker

CHAPTER 1

BEING BLUNT - BUT ARE YOU REALLY AN ENTREPRENEUR?

"An entrepreneur is an artist with business as his or her canvas."

– Leon Jay

What is your image of an entrepreneur? The guy starting a successful tech startup? Someone following a proven way to make money online? The girl opening her own shop? The person living a "million dollar lifestyle" funded from his or her passive income after attending some wealth seminar?

Forbes agrees with Dictonary.com's definition of entrepreneur: "a person who organizes and manages any enterprise, especially a business, usually with considerable initiative and risk."Prepare yourself because this is where I get my pet peeve about the business world off my chest...

I am sick and tired of hearing every business guru out there preaching that everyone should become a business owner. I know it may sell more books for them, however...

They shouldn't.

In the same way, not everyone should trade the forex, climb the property ladder, invest in stocks, or follow any other "proven" path to wealth.

Many of the "gurus" out there are teaching that every man and his dog should become an entrepreneur. Their premise is often that, as an employee, you are somehow inferior, a sucker, and doomed to financial hardship.

I don't think they mean for this to be their message—but after having spoken to countless fans of these books, courses, and seminars I get the impression this is the subconscious conclusion many people are left with.

I am here to tell you this is a big, steaming pile of horse doo-doo. (Just a personal opinion of course.)

For a start, the only way an entrepreneur can build a real business is with employees. Without employees, we are nothing. One is simply not better than another.

Now it is true that your potential income can be much higher as a business owner. It is also true that you are likely to be broke and struggling for a long time before you see that "fortune." If you ever do.

I will repeat the final five words of that definition for being an entrepreneur: "with considerable initiative and risk." I may be wrong, but I do not believe that this level of risk is for everyone.

Another truth (as we will discuss in the next section) is that money does not bring happiness past a certain (relatively low) point. Your motivation for creating a business should be greater than just money alone.

Also, 98 percent (yes, a made up stat—but from my observations quite accurate) of business owners are not "free." I also believe that "freedom" is relative and highly overrated.

Let me explain…

I am an entrepreneur.

Why?

Because I am unemployable. Simple as that.

I have the background and personality that make my work choices so limited that any recruitment agency would throw their hands in the air with despair and give up on me.

On the flipside, I also have a personality that is comfortable taking risks, requires little in the way of financial security, loves to create new things, and is a total control freak (not so beneficial—but often comes with the territory). Further, I am self-motivated, self-driven, and have learned over time to have faith in myself.

I am not in business because I think business is a get-rich scheme or because I think it will solve my depression or provide me a way out from the proverbial rat race. (I know many business owners that are far more entrenched in the "rat race" than the people they employ.)

No. I am an entrepreneur because it is who I am. Plain and simple.

Every successful business owner I know has done the hard yards. And by hard I mean harder than most employees will ever realize is possible. Ten to sixteen plus hours a day, six or seven days a week, no (or very cheap and short) holidays for years on end, putting their entire financial life on the line, living on pot noodles, and many losing relationship after relationship, all to get their business off the ground.

Elon Musk, (co-founder of PayPal, Tesla, Solar City, and SpaceX and worth an estimated eleven billion dollars) for example, reportedly worked at least one-hundred hours per week for over fifteen years. This works out to an average of fourteen and a half hours a day, seven days a week. Not a healthy example but you get the idea.

For me, an entrepreneur is an artist, with business as his or her canvas.

Like other artists, they will invest their last dollar into their art. If they sell a CD or a painting, the money goes back into furthering their development as an artist. Buying more materials or upgrading their instruments, etc.

Artists, like entrepreneurs, are often romanticized by the media, movies, and society in general.

The reality is, as with other artists, many entrepreneurs remain broke for many years. That is until they find a way to support themselves and hopefully, eventually, find that break that will put them into the successful minority.

Now, it does not have to be that extreme, but it does help.

Why do I say all this? It is like the biggest anti-sell for the rest of this book.

Because it saddens me to meet dreamer after dreamer who has been sold the dream but has not been told the reality of achieving it. I am here to tell you there is no shame in keeping a nine-to-five job.

Statistically, you will have far more free time in the short-term. And given the statistics on the number of startups and businesses that fail, you may be better off financially both in the short- and long-term.

You must realize that all the success stories you read in the media distort our vision of reality. The reason they make the cut as a story is because they are an exception and not the rule. In addition to this, the media will often focus on the highlights and make it appear to be a faster, easier, and bigger success story.

They will glaze over the years invested into making mistakes, the money that was borrowed and lost, the endless nights of frustration, the stress of competition or lack of revenue, the percentage given away to investors, or the percentage of revenue being spent on staffing or advertising.

At the time of writing, even Pandora, Yelp, and Twitter have yet to turn a profit, and Amazon just posted losses of just over half a billion dollars. It is not in the media's best interests to tell the full story, and as such, it leaves many new entrepreneurs overly optimistic.

However, if you are like me, then having the comfort of a nine-to-five job is simply not an option. If, like me, you are destined to create things from the ground up, then you are in for a rollercoaster of a ride.

You will experience the greatest hardships, the biggest stress, and headaches like you won't believe, as well as the biggest joys, greatest pride, and if you are lucky, a bright financial future.

Much like having a child, starting a business will be full of ups and downs. But in the end, like most proud parents, a true entrepreneur would have it no other way.

Now, back to the concept of "freedom"…

It is interesting to me that the greatest success stories in business are people who continue to work long after they could have retired and become "free."Think about it for a minute.

Elon Musk, Richard Branson, Donald Trump, Bill Gates, and any other self-made multi-billionaires you can think of could have retired years ago. But they didn't. (Not to say some, like Bill Gates, don't eventually. But when they do, it is to substitute their job to pursue another bigger purpose—not to lie around and do nothing.)

Cynics may say that is because greed knows no limits. But I believe it is the love for what they do that drove them to that degree of success in the first place. Steve Jobs gave it his all until his last dying breath, long after he knew he was going to die. This was dedication to his business, not the pursuit of greater wealth.

The longest living community in the world is in Okinawa, Japan. The Okinawans have no word for retirement. They do have a word, ikigai, which translates as "the reason for which you wake up in the morning."What a different mindset that is!

We are sold the idea that, if we have our business, we can throw away our alarm clock. The implication being because we don't have to get up if we don't want to.

I am here to tell you that it is true; you will know you are on the right path when you can throw your alarm clock away. But not because you don't have to get up. Instead, it is because you are so excited about what you need to do that day you will automatically wake up like a five-year-old at Christmas.

If you have a job of worth, or you run a business, you have responsibilities. (This is true, of course, if you are managing a family, too.) With responsibility comes a decrease in freedom.

So many students tell me they want to build their own business because they want freedom. Again, this is a nasty myth that is circulating due to one too many "make money" sales letters and one too many misguided personal development books.

The logic is that money brings freedom of choice. Freedom of choice brings happiness. Yet, in his inspiring TED talk, Harvard professor of psychology, Dan Gilbert, demonstrates that increased choice decreases happiness. Not just that, but within twelve months, a first prize lottery winner and someone who just became a paraplegic returned to the same baseline of happiness.

Yes, I know. It is very counter-intuitive that a paraplegic with all his hospital bills and a multimillionaire will be as happy as each other within a year. But that's what the data shows us.

Freedom is relative. Perhaps freedom is more a state of mind than anything else.

If you live a life where you are truly free of any responsibility, then, in my mind, you are living a life without purpose or meaning. (Even a monk has responsibilities and commitment to his practice.)

So many people are chasing the impossible or, at the very least, a false god.

I believe many people would be far happier embracing their job and finding meaning in their work instead of buying into a Hollywood fantasy. At best, freedom in the physical world can be defined as the ability to choose what you commit to.

If you can find peace in a good honest nine-to-five job, and know that the level of risk, responsibility, and insecurity in running your own business is not for you, then I say "good on you." I am sure the engineers at Tesla would have it no other way. They have well-paying jobs and are doing something that they love and that is contributing to making a difference in this world. How many "make money online followers" can put their hand on their heart and say the same?

Never let anyone tell you that a job is a bad choice. That is for you alone to decide. For some people, it is; for most it isn't. (So long as you are paid well enough, appreciated in your work, do something you enjoy, and work for a company you believe in. If not, then maybe it is time to change jobs—not start a business.)

If you don't agree with me and you want to keep chasing the "it's easy to make money" promise made by so many online courses or multi-level marketing companies, then no problem.

Go back to buying shiny object after shiny object*. There are plenty of people out there more than happy to keep selling you the dream and taking your money.

Now, all that said, if you are prepared to get real…if you still know that you could never work for someone else, are prepared to do what it takes, and you have no doubt that being an entrepreneur is your calling, then read on…

*I am not saying some training programs won't make you money. Some will. None of them are ever suited to everyone though. Plus, they almost always make it sound like it is easier, costs less, and takes less time than is realistic.

CHAPTER 2

THE FIVE PS OF PRIORITY

"A business that makes nothing but money is a poor business."

– Henry Ford

I have spent the past few years speaking to seminar participants and to customers at our café and co-working space for digital nomads (people who travel the world while making money online). I cannot tell you how frustrating the conversations have become over time.

Not because the people I am talking with are stupid. Far from it. The frustration comes from the realization of how many people are asking the same wrong questions, in the same wrong order. And all because that is what they have subconsciously been taught to do by the many get-rich schemes out there.

If you want to reach an end goal as quickly and as efficiently as possible, many experts will agree it is important to ask the right questions. However, equally important is asking those questions in the right order.

It took me years to realize the implications of asking questions out of their optimal sequence. It turns out the answers you get to a series of questions are profoundly different by changing the order in which you ask them.

Most people I spoke to started by asking the question, "How can I make money?" This may be quite normal, but it is far from optimal. Answering this question for someone is like trying to tell them the best person to marry without knowing the first thing about who they are.

If you are set on being an entrepreneur, I believe there are five questions that should be considered as a foundation. And the order in which you ask these questions is critical to getting the best answer.

I will explain in more detail shortly, but first, the five questions in the right order…

1. **Purpose** – What is the purpose my business will fulfill?

2. **Passion** – What is my personal passion and skill? That is, what do I bring to the business and where do I fit in?

3. **People** – Who else do I need on my team to achieve the primary purpose?

4. **Place** – Where is the best place for the business to be located?

5. **Profit** – How will the business make money?

I believe the reason so many people fail, struggle, or are unhappy is because they don't ask all of these questions, and when they do, they do not ask them in the correct sequence.

Let's run through a scenario…

If you start by asking how to make money, then every man and his dog will line up to give you an answer (for the right price of course—or worse, unqualified, well-meaning, free advice).

Many of the solutions have very well-written sales copy that narrows your focus and discredits other options. They promise you their method will make you more money, quicker and easier than anyone else's way.

Let's assume you decide on one of these profit-making methods. Let's say drop-shipping. (Drop-shipping is a method of making money selling physical products that are stocked, stored, and shipped by a drop-ship company. Your goal is to find the customers and take the orders.)

This is a common favorite way to get started in business, as there is little in the way of setup costs, and you get to leverage someone else's offline infrastructure. This allows you to run your entire business online. As a business idea, it is certainly not without merit. (Though, as we will discuss later, for most it is also far from ideal.)

The next question, "place," is often skipped altogether (the assumption being that where you are is the only place to be).

For the digital nomad community, this is often one of the first questions they ask: Where is a "cool" place to be, or where are the other digital nomads hanging out?

Thinking of our scenario above, there is a big drop-ship community in Chiang Mai, Thailand. Living costs are low and infrastructure is good, so some of these digital nomads would think, let's head there.

The next question, "people," is often overlooked until way too late in the process. But if it is asked in the planning stage, it is typically asked in the wrong way.

Many Internet business experts recommend outsourcing and trying to use the cheapest possible labor. We will discuss in depth why this is often a bad decision in one of the coming chapters.

For now, though, we have found ourselves in Chiang Mai doing drop-shipping, so we need to hire some writers to create SEO content for us (a key component of the drop-shipping model). The problem is that good English writers are hard to find in Thailand, so we must hire Filipinos via an outsource website.

This is what the courses recommended, after all.

The problem here is that many outsourced workers are poorly qualified, so finding good ones can take time. Secondly, they rarely have any loyalty, as they have no emotional connection to you or to your business and are happy to work for whoever pays them the most.

The other people you have now surrounded yourself with are working on similar projects, so they can often (not always) be more secretive than supportive. Rarely are they collaborative.

At this point, the question asked may be "What is my passion?"

The available options to answer this question will be very limited by this point. Due to the choice of business there are only so many roles that are required. These will likely exclude what someone is actually very good at, or really enjoys doing.

Following on from our drop-shipping scenario, we may find that we are left with researching niches and products. Worse, we could be spending much of our time doing backlinking or other search optimization activities.

Most people I know find this painful and boring. More often than not, it doesn't fit someone's natural core talents and is far from inspiring.

At the end of all this, we now need to find some type of purpose to explain the reason for the good percentage of our waking life.

The way to decide which product to drop-ship is chosen based by calculating demand versus competition. Hardly a decision based on a higher purpose.

Many of those who choose this path eventually find themselves working more hours and making less money than they did in a nine-to-five and delivering less value to the world when all is said and done.

In addition to all this, the reputation and survival of the "business" they have built relies on their drop-ship supplier and on Google's search results. Neither of which I would recommend. (Drop-shipping often has such low profit margins it is hard to compete using paid traffic.)

After months of trying to make it work, they become bored and disillusioned and go seeking for the next big thing. (Or they find the next big thing before they even make a cent drop-shipping and go chasing after the new shiny object. What makes a new shiny object? The promise of making money faster and easier than any other way you have seen before.It is a pattern I have seen play out again and again.

Now there are ways to make good use of (and money from) drop-shipping. But the decision to use this money-making method should come only when the question "how to make a profit" is asked last, not first.

This changes everything. It is possible to design your business and your life so they are in alignment with each other and in alignment with who you are.

It may require changing a few ingrained beliefs and false logic patterns and perhaps going back to the drawing board on a few things.

Don't panic though. You will learn exactly how in the following chapters. And I assure you, it will be well worth it.

Before we get more in-depth on the "Five Ps of Priority," I want you to take a step back and ensure we proceed with the correct attitude and a little more self-awareness. (It will help a lot later on.)

CHAPTER 3

AN ATTITUDE PROBLEM?

"Nothing can stop the man with the right mental attitude from achieving his goal; nothing on earth can help the man with the wrong mental attitude."

– Thomas Jefferson

You have no doubt read countless stories of people overcoming adversity to achieve success. You never hear the stories of people who gave up trying because, of course, they never succeeded.

Yet when it is us who is faced with stress, frustration, and problems that seem too big to overcome, it becomes all too easy to throw in the towel. If you are to survive the entrepreneur's journey, without going crazy or giving up, then you best be prepared with the correct attitude.

For me, there were two critical attitudes I needed to adopt…

The first was regarding survival. If you are to go the distance, you will need to embrace making mistakes. A lot of mistakes.

Failure is not the opposite of success. Indeed, it is the very essence of success.

Don't believe me? Ask Thomas Watson Jr., the second president of IBM.

When asked for his formula for success he replied, "Double your failure rate." He should know. During the 1960s, he lost twenty million dollars in "failures," but subsequently continued to make IBM a household name.

Schools are getting better, but for the most part, we are not encouraged to make mistakes. We are marked down for it or criticized. We need to break free from this limited way of thinking.

Face failure head on. Learn to not only allow, but also to encourage mistakes. Both within ourselves and within our team.

The idea that mistakes are an inherent part of success is nothing new. There are more stories and quotes on this concept alone than could fit in a single book. However, most people I meet struggle to comprehend or allow themselves to fully adopt this attitude.

The second adjustment I needed to make was to help with the "going crazy."Consider business as a game. Approach it the same way you would with any sport or activity that you enjoy and are passionate about.

When you play a game, you aim to win, but you also accept that you may lose. You can't expect to win every game or match, and if you did, it would soon become boring.

Imagine playing tennis. What if every time you hit the ball over the net you already knew that the outcome would be a guaranteed win? How long would you keep playing?

No challenge, no fun.

On the opposite side, imagine losing every game, never getting a single point. You would soon become frustrated and want to quit.

Does it mean you cannot become better with practice? Of course not. It just means you need more practice, a bit of coaching, and to play against someone more your own level.

A professional athlete only gets to be a professional through hard work, discipline, focus, determination, a lot of passion, and many, many losses. If you want to become a professional of anything, then be prepared to do the same.

Approach business with a sense of excitement, interest, and an acceptance that, in all probability, you will lose the first few games. Even as a top professional, you are highly unlikely to win every match.

Many people love to play computer or strategy board games for relaxation. Personally, I see business in the same way. The only difference is you can win real gold coins ☺.

Given how hard and unlikely it is to make money playing any sport or practicing any art form, it is hard to imagine anyone ever really choosing these activities as a career path purely to become rich. While it is true the top achievers in any of these fields make incredible money, the chance of them doing so without natural talent, passion, and a lot of practice is extremely low.

Passion and purpose are what give people the perseverance to overcome the pain of practice until their goal is achieved.

When you embrace the challenge of the business game, then it can be much more fun and rewarding. You will develop a rich appreciation for all the rules and intricacies of business. As you improve your skill and understanding, you will also increase the level at which you play.

Just like many games, your team members will be very important. They will both dictate the level to which you can play and how enjoyable the game will be. Even a pro tennis star may play solo on the court, but off-court he or she is supported by a surprisingly large team.

This entire book is written with these underlying philosophies. Each chapter concludes with a few questions. As we have already discussed, learning to ask the right questions will give you far better answers.

Take the time to contemplate your answers for every question. By the time you finish the book, you should be thinking in a very different way.

Please read through this book from beginning to end. It is not one of those you can just dip in and out of. The logic and ideas build on each other and should be read as such.

Before we begin...

Find a good notebook and pen that you can keep handy for taking notes of key learnings, thoughts, ideas, and insights.

Preparation is key in business. Thoughts are only worth having if you can capture them and then make good use of them later. (I used to carry a notebook everywhere. Now I have a Galaxy Note smartphone that goes everywhere with me—a great investment.)

CHAPTER 4

KNOW THYSELF

"What is necessary to change a person is to change his awareness of himself."

– Abraham Maslow

To get started, it is important to know who you are. What is your past; what is your present; and what do you want for your future?

Many business owners failure is because they are trying to put themselves in the wrong position or trying to chase someone else's dream. Worse, they simply try to copy someone else's business because they can see it made money for that person, but without any real interest in that business model or niche.

Success is unique to every individual. Both in terms of what it means to them and what they need to do to achieve that success.

Personally, I define success as:

"The achievement of a defined and meaningful goal through the process of making, and learning from, sufficient mistakes to eventually attain the intended, or better than intended, outcome."

Anything outside this is just luck.

Many men and women have believed they were on the path to success, only to realize they were not happy once they attained "it." In virtually every case I know of, this unhappiness came from the pursuit of chasing money for money's sake.

There are many studies to show that money does alleviate unhappiness—but only until the point that debt is cleared and your basic bills are met. After this, money ceases to have any tangible effect on happiness or wellbeing. (For most western countries, that figure lies somewhere between $50,000 and $70,000 per year.)

Our day to day life, our contribution to society, our own sense of importance, and our self-worth are all more impactful in the pursuit of happiness and enjoyment of life. As are the practices of healthy eating, regular meditation, proper sleep, and daily exercise.

There are many ways to make money, so why not choose one that reflects who YOU are? Why not choose one that makes a difference? One that directly contributes to both society and to your happiness?

During his 2005 Stanford University commencement speech, Steve Jobs said, "Your work is going to fill a large part of your life, and the only way to be truly satisfied is to do what you believe is great work. And the only way to do great work is to love what you do."

Yet, sadly, so few people do.

The challenge, of course, is to stop being distracted by the views of others and to take the time to understand who you are and what you really want.

Too many gurus will tell you their way is the best way.

That may or may not be true for them. But it sure does not mean it is right for you. (Including the contents of this book.)

I have studied real estate investing in depth. (All up I have spent close to $20,000 just studying this method of wealth creation, including seminars, books, DVDs, and mentoring.)

There is no denying it; there are a lot of people who have made a lot of money from real estate, even me. My very first deal I made a 30 percent profit. Problem was I hated it. But hey, at least I got my money back with interest.

It may have made me money, but really I would be happier in many jobs than staying in the real estate game. It simply was not for me. Others I met were also making money, but they were actually enjoying it. They had found something that inspired them, which they were good at, and that more than paid the bills.

This was an important lesson. There are many different ways to make money. Some I have no skill at; others I have no interest in. But business resonated with me. It provided an opportunity to learn, to challenge myself, to contribute to others, and to create something new and exciting.

Even within the world of business, there are many different models, methods and strategies for creating wealth. Once again, for most, I have neither the skills nor the interest.

Understanding who I am was essential to finding the right path for me.

So this is stage one. Without it, everything that follows will have little context or will fail to be as effective as its potential (or more to the point, your potential).

Begin by taking fifteen to twenty minutes, no less, to write your story.

This is a concept I learned from Michael Margolis, so a big shout out to him for its inspiration. He has consulted for companies such as Zappos, NASA, Geenpeace, Marriott, and Bloomberg to name a few. If it good enough for them...

The process involves writing down the answer to the following questions and expanding or adding more information where you feel it is important:

What is your name?

When and where were you born?

Who are/were your parents? What did they do? What values or beliefs did they instill in you?

Where and what did you study?

What were your passions as a child?

What did you want to be when you grew up and why?

Who were your biggest role models and heroes as a kid?

Who are they now?

What is your greatest achievement that you are most proud of so far?

What things most annoy you in life?

What inspires you most in life?

What and/or who is most important to you?

What would you most like to achieve before you die?

What are your biggest strengths as a person?

What are your strongest skills?

What aspects of your business do you most enjoy?

What aspects do you least enjoy?

What would you talk all day about if people gave you the time to listen?

Why are you doing what you are doing now?

If you could do anything, what would it be?

What would you most like to be remembered for?

If you were to die tomorrow, what would you most regret not having done?

As a business owner, my most challenging task is to find the right people for the right roles. As an entrepreneur, my biggest challenge was to find the right business and the right role for me. This process can help you gain a lot of self-awareness to help in this respect.

It may sound like a pointless process. After all, surely you already know the answers to these questions. But, for most of us, we rarely take the time to stop and reflect.

Pause for thought. Ask yourself...

What is my story? What makes me who I am? What drives me? What do I really care about and stand for?

CHAPTER 5

THE PURPOSE OF PURPOSE

"He who knows how will always work for he who knows why."

– David Lee Roth, Van Halen

Years back, in a former incarnation, I was a therapist.

I was fortunate enough to have a decent reputation and, therefore, was able to charge a decent fee. This meant that many of my clients were extremely successful—financially that is.

Despite their "success" they would come seeking help to overcome a range of problems. Depression, alcoholism, sex addictions, and even suicidal thoughts.

These were mostly men in their late 40s to early 60s that had million dollar homes and expensive cars, and some even possessed the trophy wife. But no matter how hard they climbed the ladder of success, they never came closer to reaching happiness.

As they grew older and began to reflect on their lives, depression would often set in and so would the range of associated problems that accompanies it.

While there can be many causes of depression, I found that, more often than not, it simply came down to a lack of life purpose.

During their younger years, the illusion that chasing money was purpose enough would keep them motivated. Once they had made enough to realize that more money was not taking them closer to happiness, the illusion would begin to crumble.

While this may not be the most earth-shattering observation, it surprises the number of people who say they "know this" but then proceed to make money a priority.

This perhaps also explains why people's lives are statically shortened by early retirement. Josef Zweimuller, from the University of Zurich, demonstrated how life is shortened by an average of two months for each year of early retirement. After all, without purpose, what is the reason for living?

This is basically saying that everyone chasing an early retirement is also chasing an early death.

I became involved in one online debate on this subject when someone stated that I could not be aware of Maslow's hierarchy of needs. His assumption was that, if I were aware of them, then surely I would know that money was a priority in getting our basic needs met.

But this belief is based on false logic. In actual fact, Maslow's hierarchy only supports the importance of aligning purpose before profit.

To understand this better, take a look at Maslow's diagram below.

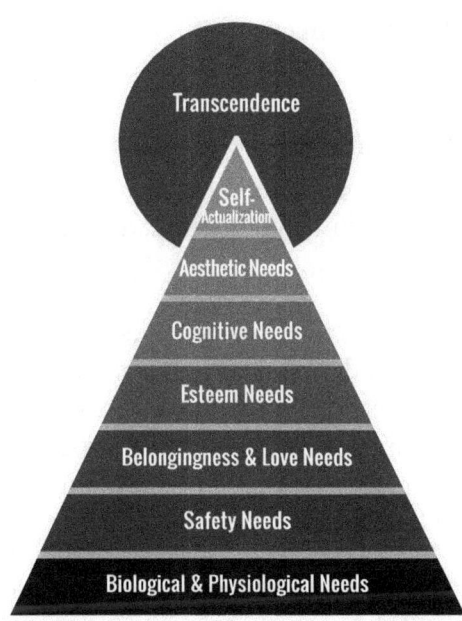

1. **Biological and physiological needs** – air, food, drink, shelter, warmth, sex, and sleep

2. **Safety needs** – protection, security, order, law, and stability

3. **Love and belonging needs** – friendship, intimacy, affection, and love—from romantic relationships, family, friends, and work colleagues

4. **Esteem needs** – self-esteem, achievement, mastery, independence, status, dominance, prestige, and managerial responsibility

5. **Cognitive needs** – knowledge, purpose, and meaning.

6. **Aesthetic needs** – appreciation and search for beauty, balance, and form

7. **Self-actualization needs** – realizing personal potential, self-fulfillment, seeking personal growth and peak experiences

8. **Transcendence needs** – helping others to achieve self-actualizationMoney does indeed help provide the first two stages and may assist with levels three and four. And these are very important.

The false logic lies in the belief that there is only a very limited number of ways for each individual to achieve their financial needs. It also assumes that you need to complete the base level stages first before considering the higher levels. (This is probably due to the way Maslow's needs are represented in a pyramid and the way our minds typically think in a linear way.)

However, from my observations, what usually happens is that, when people become focused on meeting their base level needs, they do so in a way that actually traps them from easily moving on to meeting their higher needs.

Think about all the people who are stuck in jobs they hate. They often have low self-esteem, and it is difficult for them to find meaning from the majority of their day. All too often they don't have time to spend with their family or contributing to their community.

While this type of job, business, or lifestyle may have met their short-term objectives (pay the rent and other bills, eat, and support a spouse or children), it can be next to impossible to focus on the more important aspects of life. They become dependent on the money they are now making. The fear of losing this security now prevents them from seeking a better path.

If we can become aware of this dilemma, then we can start asking better questions.

There are many paths to making sufficient money to meet your base needs, but only a few have the potential to move you to the next level. And there is no "one size fits all" answer. Each person will have his or her own potential paths.

So instead of asking, "How do I make money?" You could ask, "What will bring meaning to my life, and how can I monetize that meaning to sufficiently meet my financial needs?"This may sound more difficult than simply looking for a way to make money. However, there are two other reasons to make purpose your first priority. And it is these reasons that will help ease your journey…

The first is that having purpose creates motivation. As an entrepreneur, you will be faced with many struggles before you reach success. The truth of this is written in every business biography you will ever read. Having sufficient purpose, reason, and motivation will be what helps you keep going when others quit.

During the 2008 financial crisis, Elon Musk nearly lost all three of his companies: Tesla, SpaceX, and Solar City. This was a guy who, by the age of twenty-eight, could have easily retired for life. Tesla, in particular, was about to go under. With less than one week's worth of money left in the bank, things looked bleak to say the least.

During this time, he hardly slept. He was working every hour of the day and night. When he did sleep, he would often wake to find his pillow wet with tears. The stress was intense, and many people would have given up. But for Elon this was about purpose, not about money.

On a personal level, he still had around forty million in the bank, so he was not about to go broke. But his company was. Like a true entrepreneur, he took all of his savings and invested into Tesla. This was during a time when no one else would. He believed in changing the world, no matter what the personal cost.

It was also this act of devotion to the bigger purpose (and not just his bank account) that leads us to the second reason purpose is king: It inspires others.

This is reason enough to put purpose as your core priority. As you build a team, your chances of success will be greatly increased if you can inspire others with your vision. You will attract better team members, and they will be more motivated to do a better job.

This may sound like a side benefit, but I can assure you this is perhaps one of the most important "secrets" to making your business grow faster, better, and with a lot more fun.

Tesla could not survive on Elon's money alone. It needed the superhuman effort and commitment from the entire team. They often slept on the factory floor and worked around the clock. This does not happen for a salary. It happens when people are committed to making a vision become a reality.

(When I read this it brought back flashes of my own dedicated team sleeping under the tables in the office prior to a launch. Once again, to the entire FusionHQ team who saw us through some of those challenging times—thank you.)

The bottom line is that, whether you are creating inspiration in your own life, those around you, the people you work with, potential investors, or prospective customers a little purpose can go a long way. Purpose gets people to care. And when people care enough, they take action.

Now I should be clear… While a purpose such as freeing the world from dependency on fossil fuels or eradicating cancer is admirable, for most people it is simply not necessary.

Your purpose could simply be to provide the best coffee in town or to ensure local people have access to organic bread. It may be to remove software headaches for schools or make others feel amazing by designing or providing great clothing or accessories.

The essential part is that you have a purpose that motivates you. Something you care about and that makes you want to improve on existing competition (assuming there is any). You want something that you will be proud of once it is accomplished.

The essential step in achieving your purpose is to define it. When you can articulate exactly what you want to achieve, it will become far easier to find the best answers to the following four Ps of priority.

If you already have a business and you feel it lacks purpose, it may not be too late. Many businesses, including my own, found or evolved their purpose along the way.

When I first started FusionHQ, it was to create a tool to make my life easier when selling information products. As we developed further, we realized it was a tool that could help thousands of other people do the same. Over time, we began to realize the challenges people faced in escaping their current jobs. We saw how they became blinded by shiny objects and the promises of a better life.

This evolved our mission and purpose to helping people make better decisions. For those we can help, we provide the tools to make those dreams become a reality.

Pause for thought. Ask yourself...

What can my business do to help or improve the lives of others?

What do I care about so much that I am willing to devote my life and my money to it in the hope of making a difference?

Why does my business exist, and what could give it even more meaning?

CHAPTER 6

PASSION VS. PROFIT
(THE GREAT DEBATE ANSWERED?)

"When you're surrounded by people who share a collective passion around a common purpose, anything is possible."

– Howard Schultz, founder of Starbucks

Howard explains perfectly why the second P of priority is passion.

Once you have a strong purpose, it becomes much easier to find your passion. And it becomes easier to help ignite passion in others (the third P—People).

Professor Melissa Cardon defines entrepreneurial passion (EP) as "A positive, intense feeling that you experience for something that is profoundly meaningful for you as an individual." This means it is your purpose that gives meaning and allows passion to become possible.

I have heard many people claim they don't know how to find passion. The chances are it is because purpose is missing from their life. If your day is consumed by a career path aimed only at making money, it really is no surprise.

On a side note, money itself is very abstract and, in itself, has little or no meaning. It is simply a tool to make the exchange of goods or services more convenient. There is no fixed amount of money in this world. Unlike the universe's energy, it can be created or destroyed. Its value is only as much as we as a society give to it.

At some deep core level, we all know this. So is it really any wonder that a life spent pursuing money for money's sake is going to lead to the feeling of a life wasted?

There is often huge debate over choosing a niche you are passionate about or one that is proven to be profitable.

In one piece of research, it was found that 60 percent of Fortune 500 companies were founded without any real business plan. The truth is most entrepreneurs go by gut feeling. They are emotional more than they are logical.

It is important to remember that your role in your business is the part you need to be most passionate about. The niche you are in should already be defined by your purpose.

So long as your niche shows reasonable potential to be sufficiently profitable, then I would go for it. (Remember you are building a business, not a hobby, so you will still need to consider its profit potential.)

You should have congruency and believe in your niche. If a niche is against your ethics, or you have no faith in the products you are working on, then it is time to change.

The danger can come when people try to make their hobby a business, so they can quit their job and do something they love. Sometimes this can be a good idea; many times it will end in disaster.

Why?

Take a passionate cook for example.

She may love cooking. Live and breathe it. Everyone tells her that her baking is the best. Why not open a bakery?

Because a bakery is a business. And a business can take the fun right out of the hobby.

Now she must cook every day, all day. She must also deal with the stresses of being a business owner. This includes logistics, marketing, legal, accounting, customer complaints, and staff management.

She could build a team to manage this, but that in itself can be challenging and time-consuming.

Sometimes a hobby is best kept as a hobby.

Other times people may be better off sticking to being an employee in someone else's business. This way, they can live without the stress of running a business and can focus on what they enjoy doing best.

As we mentioned in the first section, assuming they have a good boss, fair pay, and a good team around them, many people will be far happier in life with this than becoming a business owner themselves.

Remember, it is what consumes most of your day that you need to be most passionate about. So long as that passion is applied toward a purpose that you believe in, you are much more likely to have the stamina to keep going through the challenges that are a part of building a business.

Passion assists you in becoming more successful on a practical level, too.

Passionate people have been scientifically proven to spread that passion to others. This allows you to excite other people either to work with you, help promote you, or buy from you. Whichever way passion spreads, it is only going to help.

Plus, of course, each day is just so much more enjoyable when you are passionate about what you are doing.

To help you identify which of your passions to focus on, we turn to the hedgehog principle. (The hedgehog concept is from Jim Collins's book *Good to Great*—a worthwhile read if you have not yet done so.)

The idea being that a hedgehog will always outsmart even the most cunning fox by doing one thing and doing it well. No matter how the fox tries to attack the hedgehog, the response is always the same. A ball of impenetrable spines. The hedgehog focuses on what it is good at.

To simplify, there are three simple aspects to the hedgehog principle. Skill, Passion, and Monetization. (Or as Jim Collins puts it, "What can you be the best in the world at, what are you most passionate about and what drives your economic engine?")

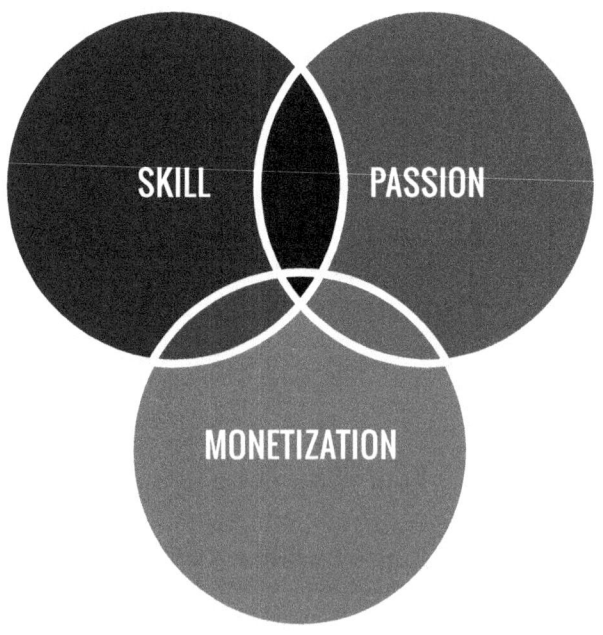

Hedgehog Principle from Jim Collins's *Good To Great*

If you can identify what you are naturally talented at, and what you enjoy doing, then chances are you will be prepared to study and practice that one thing until you become truly great at it. This is the process of mastery.

Your only challenge then is to find a way to monetize that skill.

If you have no passion for what you do, then you will never become truly great. Worse still, you will never fully enjoy each day to its full potential.

In almost every case, to monetize your skill will require a team of others. To make your business truly exceptional, each of your team members should be living their hedgehog concept, too.

Sound idealistic?

Maybe. But without its guiding light, then it is easy to go disastrously wrong.

As Chrysler says, it is more about being 'in pursuit of perfection" than actual perfection itself.

Without clarity, it is hard, perhaps impossible, to choose the best path.

We will look more at how to build a team and monetize as we proceed. They are, after all, both part of the 5 Ps (people and profit). For now, try and see how many aspects you can find that truly fit your personal passion and skill overlay.

Pause for thought. Ask yourself...

What do I love doing, and what am I really good at? For example, it may be team building, organizing, design, coding, marketing or managing numbers.

What could I contribute in making my purpose a reality, be very happy doing and find highly rewarding?

When I work as part of a team, what do I usually bring to the table?

What is the most valuable use of my time?

CHAPTER 7

PEOPLE - PAIN OR PROFIT?

"Companies are all about finding the right people, inspiring those people, and drawing out the best in people."

– Richard Branson

Peter Tiel said something very similar: "Founders are important not because they are the ones whose work has value, but rather because a great founder can bring out the best work from everybody at his company."Perhaps it is worth taking note of this wisdom. Which is why our third priority brings us to people.

If we are to be successful in fulfilling our purpose, we will need a wide range of skills to be covered. Some will be part-time positions (possibly accounting or legal), some will need to be full-time (perhaps marketing or sales). Either way, our next priority is to find the right people to build a winning team.

Because we have a purpose, and we are now clear about what we can contribute to bringing that purpose to life, it is now much easier to see which other roles need to be filled.

For example, I hate accounting (though I could do a perfectly decent job at it if I had to). I love the concept, but I am useless at coding. I enjoy design, but am not passionate enough to do it full-time or become a world expert. I can answer support questions well enough, but become quickly bored while doing it.

In my business, all of these things need doing, along with many others.

And they deserve to be done well. In fact, if I want my company to achieve success, they all need to be done very well.

There are many people out there teaching that you should "outsource" all your work. While there is a time and place for outsourcing, it should not be our first choice.

Instead, I want to find people who are highly skilled at what they do, have passion for their work, and want to align themselves with the bigger purpose. This also increases the quality of the team dynamic. It is just a lot more fun to be a part of a team that all love what they do. When a team works well together, stuff just gets done faster, better and with way less stress.

This means that, as a company, we will have a ninja team that is hard to beat. As an individual, I get to focus on the stuff I enjoy doing and am good at.

As a business owner, one of the most important things I can do is invest in building the right team. We will talk in much more depth in later chapters, as it is perhaps the most critical aspect of long-term success.

One of the most common mistakes I see new (and old) business owners make is in focusing on short-term personal profit. Essentially this means they either hire people who can get the job done (but not very well) at low rates, or they try to do it themselves to save a buck.

Trying to do everything yourself is a common entrepreneur's curse. Either due to lack of funds or, equally as common, because they are a control freak and don't trust others to do the job as well.

If you want to create passive income or a business that can be sold or a company that outlasts you, then eventually you will need to replace yourself in every task. There is no other way. Period.

I have had conversation after conversation with entrepreneurs that tell me they have tried hiring other people, and it has not worked for them. If you fall into this category, then be warned. Past failure is not an excuse for giving up and doing everything yourself.

I will tell you this…building a good team is essential. I will never tell you that it is easy.

That said, if you are having problems, it usually comes down to one of the following:

- Looking in the wrong places or hiring the wrong types of people

- Not being clear enough about what roles you need filling

- Not being willing to give people what they deserve or make them feel important

- Your business lacks real purpose or vision

- Poor communication and lack of clarity

If you want your business to keep growing, not only do you need to replace yourself, but you also need to replace yourself with people who are better than you.

At this stage in the process, you are unlikely to need a huge team. By definition, a team can be as small as two people (though it will most likely grow as your business grows).

Indeed, when starting out, it is recommended that your first one or two team members are your business partners.

It is no coincidence that many venture capital firms have learned to throw out all applications made by an individual. They know their numbers, and the statistical chance of success is so low it is not even worthy of consideration.

Think about that for a moment. It is a sobering thought.

Even from my own experience, I have started many businesses. Only those that were started with a business partner have ever succeeded (though not all). On the other hand, all my attempts to start a business alone have ended in failure. One hundred percent of them.

Of course, there are always exceptions to every rule. But in business, the odds of success are already stacked against you from day one. Why make them even worse?

Having the right team (ideally a partnership) early on will help in several ways…

Firstly, you will have at least one other person to help balance your skill set and allow you to achieve much more at a higher level on a smaller budget.

Secondly, you will have someone to bounce ideas off. This can be great for helping find possible flaws in your thinking or see opportunities you may have otherwise missed. I always find that two or more minds are better than one in generating the best ideas.

Thirdly, you will have access to a larger network of people. The quality and size of your network will prove invaluable more often than not.

Fourthly, you can get more done quicker. All things being equal, one person simply cannot achieve the same amount as two in the same time frame. To continue pointing out the obvious…this means money will arrive quicker.

Finally, and most importantly for many, you will have someone to hold you accountable.

Imagine an organizational chart. On it are all the roles that your business needs filling, no matter if it is occasional, one-off requirements; part-time roles; or full-time positions. It may look something like this…

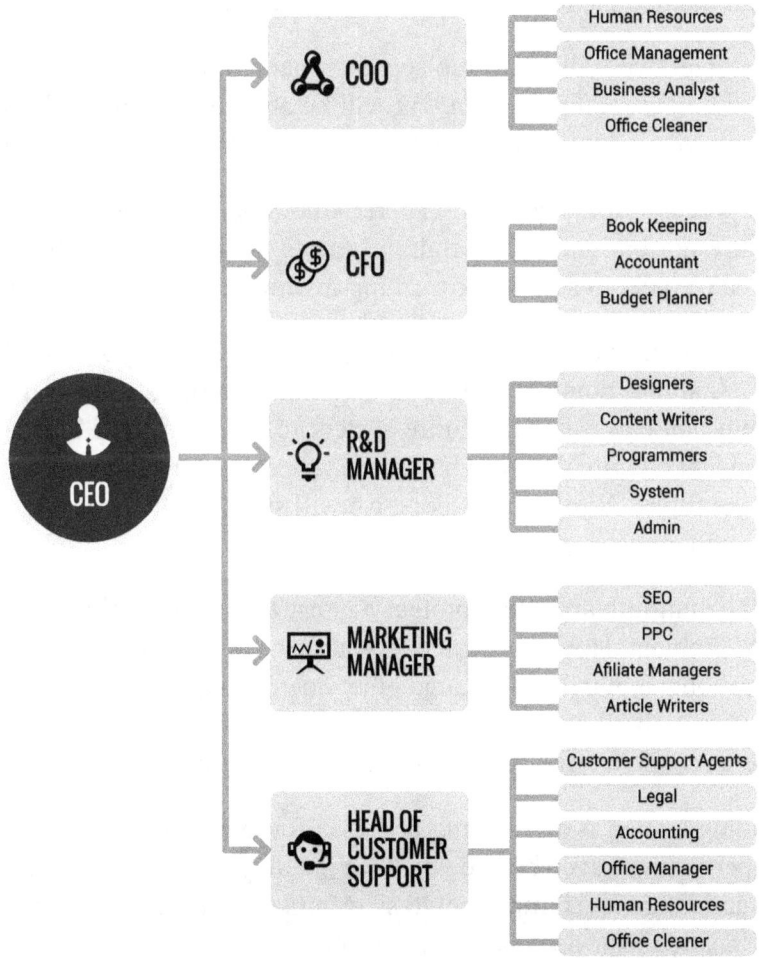

Now go through this chart and overlay the number of hours that will need to be spent to do a good job completing the tasks required of that role. You will probably want to at least double the numbers in your estimations. In the case of programming times, triple them.

Next, add the name of the person who will fill the responsibilities of each role. If you see only one name on that chart (yours), you may start comprehending the madness of it. Especially as these estimates do not include the learning time for any skills you currently lack.

Your objective will be to replace each name on that chart until you are no longer required. Then you will be able to work in the business because you want to, or you will be free to start your next project.

This process won't do itself. There is nothing accidental about it. If you are not consciously spending time to achieve exactly this, then you can expect to stay stuck working in your business indefinitely.

You also represent the biggest single point of failure to your own business. A single point of failure is a technical term for one part of a system that can cause the entire system to break. If your business is dependent on you, then you have a very weak system. No one can predict the future. While we all hope we will stay healthy and well, there are no guarantees.

Establishing a team helps protect against this single point of failure (you) problem. How you structure your team will also play a big part. Operational manuals, SOPs, and other documentation, as well as good software, will all help. This all can sound very boring, which is why I have someone on my team to take care of it for me.

Building a team is an ongoing process. You won't achieve it in a day and perhaps not even before you have put all your other four priorities into action. But it is important to start thinking who else you need that will balance your personality, skills, and resources.

Perhaps you already know who they are. Maybe you are only just realizing the value in starting to think bigger than yourself.

Either way, it is also worth noting that, despite many personal development gurus teaching "pay yourself first," in my experience, it is actually the business owner who gets paid last. Not to say you should not make any money, but your priority should be in building and supporting a dedicated team before buying yourself that luxury car.

(In his book, *Leaders Eat Last,* Simon Sinek explains this concept in much more detail. It is not just business leaders, but even generals in the army. To build a hardworking, trusting, and loyal team, put others first.)

The essence of this chapter can be summed up as this: If you want to make a small amount of fast cash then put profit before people. If you want to make a large amount of money through building a successful long-term business then put people before profit.

As I mentioned, we will look at team building in more detail shortly. Additional worksheets to assist in this process can also be found in the online training that accompanies this book. You can access them here: www.createautomateaccelerate.com/resources.

Pause for thought. Ask yourself...

What tasks and responsibilities would I prefer someone else do?

Would I prefer to work with cheap labor or experts?

How and where do I find people who are committed to my purpose, passionate about what they do, highly skilled, and who will increase the quality of my team?

CHAPTER 8

FINDING A HOME

"Location is the key to most businesses, and entrepreneurs typically build their reputation at a particular spot."

– Phyllis Schlafly

It may sound a little odd to consider the place if you are doing business online, but as they say in real estate, it is "location, location, location." Indeed, where you choose to establish your business, no matter if it is online or offline, could make or break it. This is what makes place our fourth P of priority. Let me explain…

Years back, when I decided to start to go it alone after working at Mark Joyner Inc., I had a tough decision to make.

I was living in one of the most expensive neighborhoods in New Zealand; I had just bought a new car with high monthly repayments; and to top it off, my daughter was about to turn four. I was sure of two things though…

One, I was not working for anyone else again. I wanted to build my own business. Two, I could not afford to do it where I was, especially if I were to build a team. A radical change was needed.

In under an hour, the decision was made. We would sell everything and move to Thailand. I had only visited Thailand once years before, and only for a week or so. Even so, it was just under four weeks from making that decision to flying over the Pacific Ocean to start a new, and as yet unproven, business.

Perhaps the decision seems rash to some. However, the priorities were clear, and it was the choice that made the most sense.

Thailand has good, clean infrastructure; the people are very friendly; labor and cost of living were cheap (certainly compared to NZ); the climate is warm; and in general, it is a very safe place to live. Chiang Mai, in particular, offered international schools and all the mod cons of western living on a fraction of the budget.

After years of working with unknown outsourcers, I knew I needed to build a team in person, and it is a decision I believe paid off. Relocating allowed me to use the savings I had to survive much longer and to invest in a team I could not have otherwise afforded.

Let's be clear though; moving to Thailand is not for everyone.

There is a reason why many very successful companies choose Silicon Valley as their base. Despite the higher costs, they have access to excellent talent and a network of very influential people. For others, their home and surrounding friends and family are their priority, regardless of the potential cost to the business.

As a result of spending so much time in Thailand, I have met many people who choose to build a business online and do so while traveling the world.

I should mention that, while you can build an income doing this, I rarely meet anyone who builds a successful long-term business in this fashion. Building a team and creating a routine of focus appears to be far more beneficial. The freedom to travel can certainly come once your business is automated, yet few people achieve it while in a state of perpetual travel.

As always, there are exceptions to every rule.

The majority of those that do make money while on the road are doing so by freelancing their time as designers, coders, writers, and SEO experts. Or they have created some low-level income stream just sufficient to keep them moving from one place to the next. The vast majority that have built a sustainable business have done so by staying in one place for a prolonged period of time.

Books, such as *The Four-Hour Work Week,* have become popular but are often misleading. Tim Ferris, for example, built his business first and only talked of taking "extended vacations" and managing his business for four hours a week during these vacations.

Your location may already be defined by earlier priorities such as purpose or people. Depending on what your core purpose is, or the people you may need to help you achieve it, you may have little choice in where you base yourself (or your business).

I can't stress strongly enough the advantages of working in person with other team members. This is why place should be the fourth priority and not the first.

Working together has many advantages that need to be balanced with cost, convenience, and idealism (i.e., where you would like to be). I found the speed and focus that was achieved by being in the same room with my team makes so much difference it is hard quantify.

For example, if I see a designer going down the wrong path, I can stop him or her immediately without wasting hours or even days before course correcting. By all being on the same time zone, it means no one has to wait for a twelve to twenty-four hour period to pass before getting a reply back from another team member.

Over the course of months and years, this level of efficiency adds up. (Or conversely these delays compound and project results take way longer than needed.) There are, of course, many situations when you may need to build a team remotely, and the pros may end up outweighing the cons. You just need to be aware that sometimes you may be making decisions based in a false economy.

Even if you are locked to a specific location, you may want to consider the possibility that your business may not be.

It depends on your business model, how you take payments, where your team and customers are based, and in which country you are a resident. You may consider registering your company, or having your office, in a different location than you are.

There are many regions that have different tax advantages for international companies. The Seychelles, British Virgin Islands, and Hong Kong are all well known for their zero percent corporate tax. However, other countries, such as New Zealand, offer zero capital gains tax, which is great if you plan to sell your business.

I am no international tax expert, and every case will be different. However, I can tell you it is well worth researching your options. You could save a significant amount of money by getting the proper advice. It is generally much easier to structure things properly from day one than to try and fix things later.

Ultimately, the location of you, your business, and your team will make an impact on your end result. So consider carefully and think through the knock-on effects of your decision.

Pause for thought. Ask yourself...

Where are the best people to work on my project located?

What is important to me about where I choose to live?

Where would the most advantageous place to locate my business be?

CHAPTER 9
PROFIT COMES LAST (BUT NOT LEAST)

*"Between calculated risk and reckless decision-making lies the
dividing line between profit and loss."*

– Charles Duhigg

Just because we consider profit last on our priority list, it is important to emphasize it is still a priority. And, at a logistical level, for the basic survival of your business, it is perhaps the most important of all.

A common mistake is to believe that there is a "best way to make money. People consistently search for that "way," and when money does not come, they blame the method they are using. There are many companies that adjust their profit model as their products or industries evolve.

Consider software...

Since software began, it has traditionally been sold like most products, i.e., with a single fee. While this is still a popular choice, there has been an increasing move toward many of the other possible methods to make it profitable. These include:

- Subscription-based models where customers pay a recurring fee for access

- Distributing it free and monetizing the software through advertising

- Giving the software away free to add additional functionality to hardware (which is sold to generate the revenues)

- Selling data collected (such as personal information, email address, and/or usage)

- Upselling premium content such as training, plugins, or additional functionality

- Collecting leads and following up with an autoresponder and promoting affiliate offers

- Bundling partners' products (such as a browser toolbar or trial to another software or service) and getting paid per lead sent

- Selling additional services such as hosting, premium support, coaching, or "done for you" services such as graphic design, setup, or customization

- Taking a commission from products or services sold through the software platform

- Selling the code outright, or licensing it to another company

- Embedding spyware into the software (not recommended!)

And I am sure there are more I have missed or that will develop over time.

The point is that, off the top of my head, there are eleven ways to monetize software, and that's in addition to the traditional "just sell it" approach.

It is not just software that can benefit from this level of creative thinking.

Digital information can also be monetized in many of the same ways as software. Even physical products have more flexibility than many people realize.

Electronics companies have long created as much, and often more, profit from selling extended warranties than they do selling the hardware. One car yard I read about would sell cars at zero profit. They dominated their local area because other competitors were too afraid to sell cars at, or even below, cost. The car yard would then make its money with all the add-ons (premium wheels, leather seats, sunroof, insurance, and extended warranties, etc.)

Physical books, too, are no stranger to hidden ways of generating revenue. You could include affiliate or CPA (cost per acquisition, i.e., getting paid per lead sent) links to related products or services, add upsells to coaching, sell advertising space in the resources section, have a paid community on the back end, collect leads from the book and follow up with them, sell franchise rights (think Rich Dad Poor Dad), sell resell rights, or license your content...

Many companies now use an expanded approach to monetization. They will use a combination of the above suggestions to increase their revenue. For example, it is not uncommon for many companies to sell their base product on subscription, upsell premium support or functionality, sell customers' information, and embed affiliate offers or free trials to other companies' products.

Most people are not even aware of just how much money these companies are making behind the front-end transaction.

Some of the biggest companies in the world started out with no idea how they were going to make money. Take Google for example...

They started out with a purpose to make the world's information available with a single click. They were passionate, talented programmers who found a way to make this happen. They attracted a lot of additional talent because their enthusiasm was contagious and their purpose exciting. Fortunately, they were already based in the right place to find high-end talent. When they finally decided to try and make some money, the original idea was to try to sell their technology to Yahoo.

Yahoo did not want it, so they needed to come up with another solution. They never started out with the intention of becoming one of the world's largest advertising networks. They started out with the idea to be the world's greatest search engine. Profit came last but was ultimately essential for the company to survive, then thrive.

Since then, of course, they have branched out to create many different revenue sources. This was much easier because the profit model was not central to their business plan. Had they built an advertising agency, the profit diversification would have been possible, but a lot more limiting.

The important thing to realize is that there are many ways to generate a profit from almost any product or service. It is a very important consideration, but as you can see, by leaving it to last, you get more options, not less.

You will also have designed a business you are enthusiastic about that provides value to others and makes you proud. And along the way you can also become very wealthy (without selling your soul to the devil!)

We will continue to explore business models and how to integrate many of the ideas discussed in this chapter. For now, though, put some thought into how you may apply each of these methods for monetization to your business.

Pause for thought. Ask yourself...

What ways are my competitors are monetizing their business?

How do other industries monetize their businesses, and what can I learn from this?

What ways can I monetize my own business and fund the achievement of my company's purpose?

CHAPTER 10

THE BONUS P

"I don't design clothes; I design dreams."

– Ralph Lauren

I want to address another P, product, as an extension to profit.

For the purpose of this chapter, I will treat a product or service as the same thing.

There are many people who teach a business model focused on one specific product, e.g. a Kindle book or selling t-shirts. Based on the results of your five priorities, you may have found that a product is not even required (for example, if you will use advertising, licensing, or affiliate products to generate your revenue).

Chances are, though, you will want to sell a product, if not now then later.

In some businesses, the product is central to everything. It is the medium through which the company's purpose can be met. If, like Percy Shaw, your purpose is to prevent deaths from car accidents, then the product may well be the focus of the business. In his case, the cat's eyes or reflective road studs we now see in the center of roads around the world, were the core of his business.

The cat's eye was the solution to the problem. Same for Google search and Solar City. The products are the solutions for achieving the company's purpose.

Of course, getting your product accepted and adopted by the market is another story. This will make up much of your sales and marketing efforts. There is always more to a business than just making a great product.

If your mission is to spread an idea, a concept, or life changing information, then there are many mediums through which you can do this. In this example, you may consider creating books, videos, audios, podcasts, videos, TV shows, radio shows, webinars, seminars, retreats, or workshops.

You have to remember, when spreading an idea, the form you deliver your information in is not really your product. Your content is. The form you put it in is just a way to package, deliver, and monetize that content.

When your product is the vehicle to make your purpose a reality, you will want to make it the best product you can. If you are filled with enthusiasm and have a good team around you, then this will be much easier. However, you also need to accept that nothing great starts out as great.

Greatness comes from a process of constant feedback, refinement, and improvement. And this takes time (as well as a huge degree of patience, a lot of mistakes and a bucket-load of humility).

You may have heard of the MVP (minimum viable product), a concept popularized by Eric Ries in his book *The Lean Startup*. The idea is simple. Get your product to market as quickly as you can. Within reason of course.

Many entrepreneurs (and companies) try to make their products perfect and feature-rich before launching. Only to find that the market did not want what they had or had different requirements than the founders originally anticipated.

By getting a basic working version into the hands of a few customers, you can use their feedback to test and refine. This also gives you the chance to scale in a manageable way.

Rather than repeat the contents of Eric's book here, if you are indeed doing product development, then I would suggest you go read up on MVPs.

At the end of the day, the idea is not to produce low-quality products. It is to use a deliberate process to get the feedback you need in the real world to eventually produce something that you can be proud of. Something that achieves your initial purpose. Something that is truly great.

For other businesses selling products, is just a way to monetize your business so that you can fund your bigger purpose.

Think of an animal rescue center for example. They will often sell pet supplies, "sponsor an animal" programs, t-shirts, or fluffy toys and other merchandise. They are not in the business of producing furry toys, nor do they have a passion or interest in the manufacturing or even the retailing of pet food or children's stuffed friends.

Their mission is to save distressed animals and find them homes or release them back to the wild. But this takes money. The products they sell are merely the way to monetize their business.

That does not mean they should not take pride in the products they choose to stock. Items should still be of a decent quality and relevant. But you see, the focus of the business model is very different. The products sold are secondary, not the heart and soul.

There is no right or wrong here. Just different ways to approach the same big picture objective. That is to create a viable business that you love and which has meaning.

It is important to understand the different approaches from the big picture perspective. This way, you can better evaluate which product or business advice is applicable to you.

Pause for thought. Ask yourself…

Is my product the core of my business or just a way to fund a bigger purpose?

Which product or service is most appropriate for us to sell?

CHAPTER 11

GAMOPHOBIA

"I fear not the man who has practiced 10,000 kicks once, but I fear the man who has practiced one kick 10,000 times."

– Bruce Lee

Gampohobia is the fear of commitment.

Here comes the part that most entrepreneurs I know struggle with. However, if you have your 5 Ps of Priority in order, this should be considerably easier.

For most of my life, I have not been able to focus on one project for more than a couple of days. My mind would be coming up with new ideas all the time. And new ideas are generally more exciting than old ideas. And focus will generally follow excitement.

The problem is, there is no such thing as a million dollar idea. Only a million dollar implementation. And implementing takes longer than the creation of new ideas.

There is another very powerful force at play, constantly pulling you away from success. This force enhances the lure and temptation of new opportunities. It is one of the strongest drivers of human behavior, known to all good copywriters, salespeople, and psychologists.

The chances are it has influenced many of both the small and big decisions throughout your life.

It is the fear of loss. Or more specifically, in the entrepreneur's world, the fear of missed opportunity.

Perhaps, ironically, the fear of loss is one of the biggest factors leading to unattained potential. Even more ironic, perhaps, is that the more desperately someone needs to succeed, the greater risk they have of falling prey to this slippery demon.

How so?

Well, if you are short on cash, then chances are you are on the lookout for every possible opportunity to make money. The fear kicks in when saying no to any opportunity that presents itself. What if that was the big break? What if that was the answer to your troubles? What if you are currently chasing the wrong path that is leading to nothing?

You can't afford to lose it. Or so you tell yourself.

As desperation builds, so does the fear. Fear can cloud good judgment. This leads to poor decisions that lead to poor actions further leading to even poorer results.

Why is it that chasing multiple opportunities is a fool's folly? After all, countless books and gurus teach us to build multiple streams of income, right?

Hmmmm. Maybe. But let's look closer…

How many people successfully built multiple streams of quality income simultaneously? The answer is only those with enough existing experience and resources to do so. I have yet to meet anyone who has achieved this starting alone or with low to no budget.

Why is this the case?

Answer: simple mathematics.

You have no doubt heard about the power of compound interest. So the question is, "If I put $1,000 into an account and added $100 each month into that one account, or split my $1,000 upfront and my $100 per month across 3 accounts (all with the same interest rates), which would net me the biggest return?"

The answer is, of course, the single account. (Based over 30 years at 10% the difference would be a total of $65,153.95 from 3 accounts vs. $214,842.23 from a single account.)

A successful business is the compounded result of thousands, or even millions, of different decisions and actions.

Charles J. Givens eloquently explains, "Success requires first expending ten units of effort to produce one unit of results. Your momentum will then produce ten units of results with each unit of effort."All of the psychological research out there has shown two very important things...

As humans, both the quality and quantity of our work decreases when we multitask. Secondly, we have a limited amount of decision-making capacity. Once we have used our daily quota, our decisions suffer greatly.

When you combine the implications of these three factors, that is power of compound results, inability to multitask, and our limited capacity to make many quality decisions, we start to see why the chance to succeed over multiple simultaneous opportunities drops to almost zero.

Imagine trying to get to even just two destinations at once. You spend a day walking toward one, then a day walking to another. Keep repeating this process, and you will never get to either—unless they are on the same route.

And there lies the critical point of difference. If you have multiple objectives and goals, they need to be in alignment with each other.

Unless they are, you will become tired and frustrated.

Now I know there are some readers that will try and pick holes in my logic and analogies.

Of course, there are variables that make building a business not as clean-cut as basic compound interest calculations. However, if you use this type of logic to argue the point, it will only be you who loses out in the long-term.

I should know. I did it for years.

I was given the same advice not long after I started online. Let's pretend for a moment that it was not explained to me as well as I have explained it to you here (so I don't appear such a fool). For the next few years, I jumped from project to project, each overlapping and most never making a cent. Those that did never came close to reaching any more than a few thousand dollars at best.

My resources were spread too thin to focus enough force to generate a decent impact.

Bruce Lee understood this. His point being that you can try and spread your time thin, learning 10,000 different ways to hit a man. But unless you properly master each one through repeated focus, discipline, and practice none of those methods are going to be that effective.

Forget the math and the logical arguments for one moment. Just look at the evidence around you.

How many multimillion dollar companies were built simultaneously by the same founder and the same team on the same budget?

Not one that I know of (and I have done a lot of research in this area).

Think of focus in terms of sight. The better you are able to focus, the more clarity you have. The more clarity you have, the better quality feedback you have from your environment, and the better decisions you are able to make.

In business, the longer you are able to focus on your business environment, the more data you will get. This will give you more information to make better-informed decisions. The result will be an improved chance to modify your environment effectively to get the results you are aiming for.

Once you have one solid product or service that is generating an automated revenue, either through the use of established teams or software, then you MAY be ready to expand your sources of revenue—one at a time.

There is no exact science for knowing when the best time to diversify your focus is, as it is impossible to predict the future. (Something that is also proven from much psychological research. Even experts, it seems, are rarely better at predicting the future than non-experts in any given field.)

Also, it is not until you have a working system that real leverage to a business can be applied. Take split testing as an example.

It is possible to spend ten minutes setting up and split testing a headline (more on this later) and double the revenue from your sales page. Now, assuming this was your only product for now, that means you just doubled your entire businesses revenue—but you have more than doubled its profits.

How so?

Because there is always a base cost that needs to be met when running a business. This means that a certain number of sales are needed just to break even. The sales beyond this threshold amount provide the actual profit.

Let's assume you are spreading your time over multiple projects. If so, you will take longer to reach both your base costs and these critical opportunities for leveraging all of the work done up until that point.

The more your business grows, the more of these leverage opportunities you will have. The more of THESE opportunities you take advantage of, the more money you can make.

I was discussing this topic with a friend of mine recently. He argued that, by keeping his options open, he had nothing to lose. However, all of the data tells us that actually he was more likely to lose by keeping too many options open.

Think of this in terms of a romantic relationship...

By keeping your options open and not committing to one relationship, you are unlikely to develop anything serious or long-term. You may have a lot of fun and excitement starting many new "projects," but ultimately nothing meaningful will come from any. At least not until you commit and focus on one.

Imagine going to an investor and , "I have four projects I am currently juggling. Could you invest in one or more of them?" Of course, an investor would laugh you out of the room.

Why?

Because he knows he would never see his money again.

Indeed, investors will rarely invest in a business where the owner is not 100 percent full-time. If they have to have a day job to fund themselves while building the business most investors will run a mile.

Now consider that most venture capital (VC) firms are used to dealing with high-risk ventures (between 79 percent and 81 percent of all companies they back fail). And VCs are less desperate to see a return on their investment than most entrepreneurs (the VCs already have enough money to eat). These investment firms cannot be sure what will work, but through experience, they are fairly confident on what won't.

When starting a new business, the odds are already stacked against you. You would have to be stupid or crazy (or crazy stupid) to go against all the statistical data and reduce your odds to almost zero. Yet people do it all the time.

(Statistically, you are likely to think you are better than average and are somehow exempt from the law of focus. Again, statistically, you likely believe that your circumstances are different, and this advice does not apply to you. Statistically, we are better at fooling ourselves than others, and statistically, if you ignore the advice in this chapter, you will be wrong.)

Focus is non-optional. It is essential.

This is one reason why the five Ps are so powerful. Assuming you have a clear purpose, you are passionate about your role in bringing to life that purpose, you have a solid team to support you and hold you accountable, you have a good location and a clear path to creating profit, then focus should become a lot easier.

That said, you will still need awareness and discipline to stay true to your chosen path.

Pause for thought. Ask yourself...

What am I focused on?

What is the one thing I am committed to more than anything else and am willing to sacrifice all other opportunities to ensure I succeed?

CHAPTER 12

WHAT DO YOU WANT ANYWAY?

"To succeed in your mission, you must have single-minded devotion to your goal."

– A. P. J. Abdul Kalam

So far, we have identified our priorities and have hopefully gotten them in alignment with who we are and made the commitment to fulfill our purpose.

Even when people are clear on their priorities, we still don't have quite enough information to determine how to structure that business.

I am asked so often "Which business model is the best?", or "What should I do first?"Both questions are impossible to answer without first understanding both the purpose of the business and the financial goal or needs of the person who is creating it.

The type and size of a business required to reach one goal can be quite different than what is required to reach another. For example…

If you are aiming to make \$400-\$1,000/month to supplement your family income, your ideal business model may be very different than someone looking to make \$4,000-\$10,000/month to support themselves. This, in turn, will be quite different than someone looking to build a company that generates \$100,000-\$1,000,000 or more each month.

Your end goal will also determine many things. Do you plan to sell your company or pass it on to your children? In both cases, the structure and branding will be important to get right from day one.

Are you looking to automate much of your business to create passive income? Most Internet businesses should be able to do this, but they don't because they are not planned or built properly from the ground up.

Are you aiming to reach as many people as possible, or to target a small audience and provide a bespoke service?

Do you want to become a celebrity in your niche? How important is public recognition to you?

All of these factors will help determine what you need to do. Yet countless people I have spoken to have no clarity on any of this. Be clear about the answers to these questions, and it will help you make many critical decisions.

There is no right or wrong in the broad sense, but there will be answers that are more right for you personally. Not everyone wants to build a big company; not everyone is content running a small solo operation.

Dare to think big, but don't think too big just because you think that a "bigger" answer would be a more "correct" answer. Your answers should represent who YOU are.

Once you are clear on these goals, you will then be able to evaluate whether any given business model will meet your needs. I have met one too many people who have spent months or years creating something that was never going to meet their objectives, simply because they had not thought it through.

For example, if your intention is to create passive income, then almost any type of freelancing business is not going to get you to where you want to go. Not unless you build a team of people who do the freelance work for you.

If you want to create a multimillion dollar company and sell out, then it is unlikely to happen with a handful of affiliate or AdSense sites.

Once again, asking the right questions and becoming clear early on can save a lot of wasted time, effort, and money.

Pause for thought. Ask yourself...

How much money do I need to make for myself?

How much money would I like to make for myself?

How much money will the business need to generate in order to keep operating?

Do I want to be well-known or recognized as an individual? If not, am I willing to become recognized if it would be beneficial to the business?

How important is the ability for the company to run itself without me?

What is the end goal for my business?

Which is the most suitable business model to meet my objectives?

CHAPTER 13

WHICH MODEL ARE YOU BUILDING?

"I tend to approach things from a physics framework. And physics teaches you to reason from first principles rather than by analogy."

– Elon Musk

What business are you in?

It appears to be an easy question, yet so few people can answer it well. (So don't be ashamed if this includes you.)

It is not surprising, really; few people are teaching this fundamental principle.

Let's be very clear, for those of you who have read one too many make money online sales letters—Internet marketing is not a business. It is a tool for doing business.

Likewise, using Facebook is not a business model (except for Facebook itself).

It is important to understand that most of the ways people teach to make money online are actually just tools to help you do business. social media, SEO, PPC, blogging, podcasting, the list goes on.

Another important point to make is the oversimplification of the terms "online business" and "offline business." Rarely is it this black and white. Most offline businesses these days have an online presence and/ or use online marketing practices.

Many online businesses have offline support teams, maintain warehouses for shipping product, use offline marketing methods in conjunction to their online efforts, or have offline teams working to create products, provide services, or develop software.

The boundaries between the two are very gray.

I think you are better off not even trying to define yourself as one or the other. Instead, define your business by its purpose. Then try to see which parts of your business are best managed online and which need to be taken care of offline.

If you limit yourself to only one or the other, you are most likely only going to limit your businesses potential.

That said, what are some common business models that work very well when more Internet-based? (Many of these may give inspiration to offline businesses on how they can use the Internet to add additional revenue or to help automate some of their operations.)

Affiliate Marketing

This is nothing more than being a commission-based salesman. The man (or woman) in the middle.

This is where you get a cut of each sale that is made by sending someone looking for a product or service to someone else supplying that product or service. Thanks to the Internet, this is easy to do and easy to track.

There are many ways to do affiliate marketing. As with each of the business models a full understanding would require at least a complete book unto itself. Here, I will just give a basic overview, so you can decide if it is something you may want to explore further.

As an affiliate marketer, you are in the business of introducing people to products or services they are either looking for or that may help them.

One big benefit of this model is that you can make money without the need to produce or fulfill a product or service. You don't need to write sales pages, and you don't need to deal with customer support.

Downside is you don't get to keep the buyers list; you don't have control over conversions or product development; and often, you don't keep such a high percentage of the sale (especially on physical products).

Digital Information Marketing

This is selling digital content to people online. Usually "how to" products.

This could be in the form of e-books, audios, videos, paid newsletters, or live webinars (an online seminar or workshop).

Some digital products are delivered directly to the buyer; others are packaged in a membership site and can be drip-fed over time.

As a digital information marketer, you are in the business of selling digital content. You may also be in the business of creating that content, but that is not always the case.

Benefits are that you can optimize the entire sales process, products are usually cheap to source or produce, and margins are high. Reproduction and delivery are practically free.

The downside is you must create or source content to sell, and you must have sales copy that actually works. It is also easy for competitors to copy your ideas and for customers to share your content.

E-commerce

For the purposes of this book, we will define e-commerce as selling physical products online.

There are many forms of e-commerce. You may be using it as a way to distribute physical products you manufacture; you may be selling products you source and stock; you may be using a distribution warehouse or a fulfillment center (such as Amazon).

This is traditionally done using an online store and often (but not always) involves having many different products to choose from.

Benefits include having a more tangible value to what you are selling, typically lower refund rates, and the ability to sell through platforms such as Amazon and eBay (which can provide a rich source of buyers).

The downside is returns are harder to deal with. Usually you must manage inventory, profit margins are lower, and you must manage shipping costs, especially with international orders.

Drop-Shipping

Drop-shipping is when someone else stocks and sends the product(s), but you take the order and manage the customer. Technically, it is more a way of managing stock and delivery than it is truly a separate business model.

It almost borders on being an affiliate model, as you are selling someone else's product, but, in this case, you are doing so through your own sales pages and merchant account, and you get the customers details.

This leads to its own unique set of pros and cons.

Benefits include not having to buy stock up front, not having to store stock, and not having to deal with post and packaging.

Downsides include lower margins, that your reputation relies on a third party, and that if the drop-shipping company goes out of business so do you (unless you can find an alternative supplier). Returns can also be more complicated to deal with—though this will vary supplier to supplier. Because the margins are lower, it can limit you to low-cost methods of acquiring customers.

Services

Service based industries include coaching, transcription, copywriting, SEO, website building, graphic design, programming, customer support, accounting, etc. The list is almost endless.

With services, there is a real value to the customer because they are getting something done for them. There is also actual work involved for each individual customer that the business owner, or the business owner's team, must fulfill. (This generally means selling time for money.)

The majority of online freelancers fall into this category.

Benefits include providing something of real value, finding a way to monetize what you enjoy doing, and often the ability to secure a repeat customer.

The downside is that you can only scale if you build a team of people to actually provide the services offered. Also, you may be in competition with people from around the world, many of whom live in countries where it is cheaper to live and are willing to do the work for less.

It may also be harder to please all your customers (think web design for example—not everyone is looking for the same thing, and managing expectations can be difficult).

Software

In many ways, developing and selling software is very similar to being a digital information marketer. The big difference, of course, is that developing software can be more time consuming and costly than building information products.

Plus, providing support, training, and ongoing updates is much more demanding.

The main benefit of software over digital information is it usually has a higher perceived value. It is also harder for others to copy your ideas (depending on how complex your software is).

The downside (apart from increased support challenges) is that it can be very costly and time consuming. Unless you are a developer, have experience in this field, or have a bucket load of money to pour into your ideas, then this model is not usually for the beginner.

Software As A Service (SAAS)

This is, in many ways, the holy grail of online business. It is also not for the faint-hearted.

SAAS companies provide services such as autoresponders, web hosting, media streaming, business management tools, affiliate tracking tools, and payment gateways, as well as many others.

These companies can provide a service that is delivered using online software, not a human. This makes the service very scalable, automated, and one that usually enjoys larger profit margins.

In most cases, monthly or yearly fees are charged, which gives the advantage of recurring revenue.

Benefits not only include scalability, automation, and recurring revenues, but the company can also become a high-value asset that can be sold.

If you think about it, companies such as Facebook, YouTube, and Google also fall under this category. The only difference with these services is that they are free, and the companies monetize through advertising (see next section).

The downside, however, is they are often tricky to setup, require a decent tech team, usually require considerable customer support, and can be costly to get off the ground. In most cases, there is also a strong degree of competition.

Advertising

There are some advertising funded businesses that fall more under the SAAS category. But for many advertisers, their business is based on creating content sites or blogs that receive high volumes of traffic, or building large lists, and then selling advertising space.

Advertising may also come in the form of sponsored blog posts, banners or text ads on the site, video adverts, a solo ads (emails sent to promote a specific product or service), a paid ad in a newsletter or embedded into free software (either downloaded, mobile apps or free SAAS sites).

The main benefit of advertising is you can provide a high-value content site, software, or service for free. This can help you build a large user base, which is also then a valuable asset in its own right.

By funding your business through advertising, you can focus on building a loyal following. Monetization is easy, as you can tap into one of the many advertising networks. This way you don't need to worry about individual contracts or direct relationships with advertisers.

The downside is that you need a significant amount of traffic to really do well. Also, many advertising based businesses rely heavily on SEO, which can be an unstable form of traffic. In addition to this, you need to be careful about over-advertising so as to avoid annoying users of your site or software.

You may have noticed by now that many businesses overlap or integrate multiple approaches. For example, most information marketers add additional revenue by also being affiliate marketers. They may also generate even more revenue through advertising.

This ties back to the different ways you can monetize your business as we discussed earlier. The important thing here is to gain clarity over the different business models and different ways you are monetizing your products and/or services. Understand which you are using, when, and why.

Already you can see there is not a perfect "one size fits all" model. But there may be one or two that are more suited to your ideas, experience, or personality.

Pause for thought. Ask yourself…

Which business models are my competition using and why?

What business models are other people using in different industries? What are the benefits of using these models, and can they apply to what I am doing?

Which is the most suitable business model, or combination of business models, for me to use?

CHAPTER 14

THE SEVEN RULES OF CHOOSING A BUSINESS MODEL

"A business is successful to the extent that it provides a product or service that contributes to happiness in all of its forms."

– Mihaly Csikszentmihalyi

Before committing to the final design or structure of your business, I want you to evaluate your ideas so far.

There are many systems for making money. In my highly judgmental opinion, only a few of them are worth the time of day. Without pointing figures at any given one, I will teach you how to decide for yourself if the one you are choosing is worthwhile.

To me, there are six simple questions you should ask of any business opportunity. (This is true both online and offline.) Your choice should be:

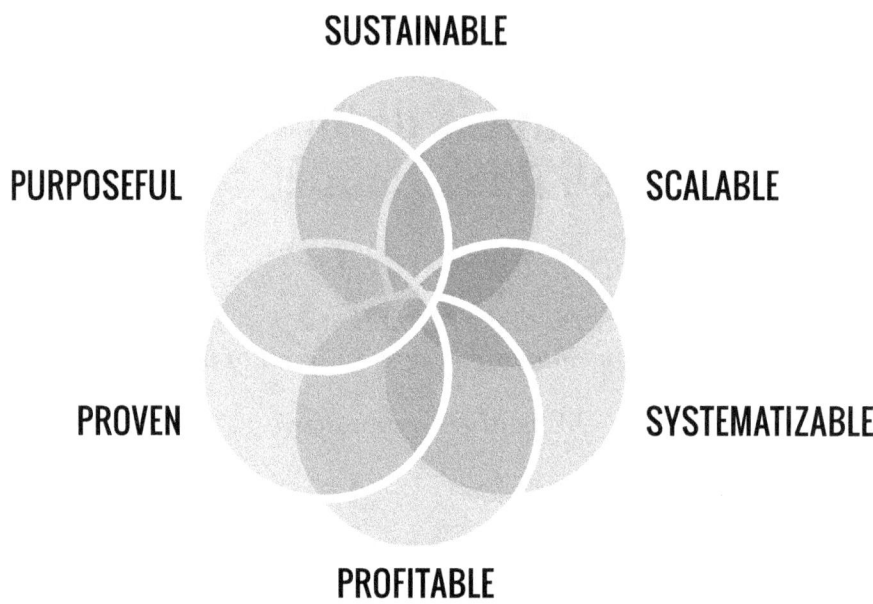

SUSTAINABLE

PURPOSEFUL

SCALABLE

PROVEN

SYSTEMATIZABLE

PROFITABLE

Sustainable

I don't know about you, but I want to know that my business will last.

Sure, nothing in this world is guaranteed, but some things are doomed to a short life from the very beginning. Businesses built on Facebook, for example, can find themselves out of business very quickly because of a change in Facebook's terms and conditions.

I have had friends that built five and six figure a month AdSense incomes. But then had their accounts suspended by Google. No warning, no getting them back.

Many of the strategies being taught rely on a loophole, current trend, or fad. Evaluate both your niche and your business model for sustainability. Spending months building a business that dies quicker than the time it took to build it is no fun for anyone.

Scalable

Every business has its limits in terms of how big it can scale. The question is, have you evaluated yours to see if it can scale to meet your financial goals?

There is no exact science around this, but being aware and realistic helps. Offline businesses can be far more limited in this regard. Once you are online, you have a global audience. Even so, here a few basic questions you should ask yourself:

- What is the size of my potential audience?

- What products or services can I provide to grow my business?

- How difficult will it be to keep acquiring new customers?

- How difficult will it be to scale my product or service?

- Once I reach this business's full potential, will I be satisfied with the result?

Almost every business owner I meet wants to scale. Yet few plan how they will achieve this. A little thought can go a long way.

Systematizable

Technically, systematizable is not a word; I know. But it should be.

This really ties into the last point. If you can systematize your business, then it becomes far easier to scale. Think of any fast food chain.

Most busy restaurants struggle to keep up with customer orders. The idea of opening literally hundreds or thousands more would fill most owners with dread. It would just be too overwhelming.

So how does any big chain manage such a feat?

Through creating systems of course. Without systems, it would be impossible.

Another phrase I hear bandied about on the

Internet and in the personal development world is "passive income." An interesting goal indeed. I know many chasing it but few with a clear plan on how it will be attained.

Let me be very clear… Owning a business is NOT creating passive income. At least not for the vast majority of business owners I know. But it can be. If, and only if, the business owner can and does systematize EVERYTHING.

There are only two ways to systematize anything that I know of. Machines and people.

Internet-based businesses can use software to program machines (computers) to do much of the work automatically. This reduces (but does not usually eliminate) the need for people.

To systematize people, you need clear roles, objectives, and procedures for them to follow.

More on this later…

Profitable

Obvious?

Maybe. But it still needs to be given consideration.

Not all products or services are as profitable as each other. And figuring how to monetize your business is an important step in ensuring its survival. If you are running on low profit margins, you will be vulnerable to undercutting by competitors.

You will also struggle with affording sufficient revenue to invest fully in lead acquisition. The larger your margins, the more you can afford to spend on marketing and building your customer base.

If you are providing services that require manual labor can you provide the service and still make the kind of income you want?

Many a business owner has created a full-time job for themselves with a capped earnings potential. You can't give yourself a raise once you reach that ceiling.

Proven

Many venture capital firms will not invest into copycat businesses. They are looking for the gamble that will pay off big. Really big.

Their odds of success are not good. Between 79 and 81 percent of all VC-backed companies die an unceremonious death. And that is with millions in funding, great networks, and experienced mentors.

If you have the money, have an idea you believe in, and want to take the risk, then go for it.

If, like most people, you want a little more certainty, then look to see if your business model has been proven. See if there is a blueprint laid out already.

I am not suggesting you simply copy someone else's business. Not at all. But companies like Facebook, Twitter, Google, etc. were huge risks, as they were unproven models. There are far more ideas like these that failed than succeeded.

There is plenty of money in building a proven business model and no shame in it. You can still be creative and expand on and improve what already exists.

You probably won't get VC funding; these guys want the potential of hundreds of millions to billions of dollars return on their investment.

That said, you are also more likely to succeed and build a business that meets the financial goals of most people.

Purposeful

You will hear me repeat this a lot. Your business should have meaning to you. Not just as a source of money.

It is no secret… for the most part, I hate the "Internet marketing" world.

I love the concepts, the strategies, the tools, and the potential to help real businesses. But I hate the vast majority of training and products. Many of the people making money in it are doing so through scamming others.

They sell low-value products, misinformation, and sometimes outright lies.

On another side note, I am also sick of hearing the BS from the personal development world. Things like "You will be rewarded proportionally to the value you provide." Nice thinking. Only wish it were reality.

The harsh truth is there are plenty of people making many a fortune by providing little to no value or straight out ripping others off. I just hope you don't become one of them. There are also plenty of examples of people providing amazing value and getting nowhere financially.

My favorite example of this comes from the Northern Hills of Thailand. In a small village, an old lady became famous for her noodle soup. Each day she would supply almost the entire village. Each bowl cost about thirty cents and tasted great. Amazing value. Only problem was her daughter later calculated it cost the lady about thirty-two cents per bowl in raw cost.

Sadly, this is a true story. One lady doing what she loved, providing amazing value, and going broke in the process. A little business sense goes a long way.

On the other hand, there are plenty of thieves, crooks, and con men providing zero value and making way more. The point is obviously not to become a criminal or avoid providing value. Just don't confuse the difference between wishful thinking and good business strategies.

However, if you want to gain far more from your business than just money, then make it purposeful.

Businesses can be socially responsible. To a very large extent, they create and shape the society we live in. They impact every one of our lives from the moment we wake up to the moment we go to sleep, and even hours in between.

Our accommodation, transport, entertainment, education, communications, health care, and the food we eat—all provided by businesses. If we want to change the world, then a business may be one of the most powerful tools we can use.

Like any tool, it can be used for good or bad. Make a decision to help people, and you will not only be able to make money, you will also be happier and sleep better at night, too.

Remember Maslow's hierarchy of needs. It is possible to take all eight levels into account when planning your business. Try and avoiding reacting to fear and making short-sighted decisions that lead to compromising your integrity.

When I come to lie on my death bed, I want to be proud of my achievements and my contributions. I trust you do, too.

Pause for thought. Ask yourself...

Do my business ideas so far meet all six criteria for a solid business model? If not, how can they be adjusted so that they do?

What can I do to increase the value my business delivers to its customers?

What can I do to ensure it is sustainable?

What can I do to make sure it is scalable?

What can I do to make it more profitable?

What other businesses are similar that are already proven? What can I learn from them?

CHAPTER 15

THE INTERNET GROWTH CYCLE

"Growth is a spiral process, doubling back on itself, reassessing and regrouping."

– Julia Margaret Cameron

Now that we have looked at possible business models, I want to give an overview to almost every business that sells information as its primary revenue. It is also used by many software companies and, if properly understood, can be used by many other businesses, too.

It is a self-circulating spiral of growth. If understood, it becomes much easier to master. Ignore it and you may find you are the one going around in circles. It looks like this…

Let's look at this in more detail.

Step 1

You will have probably heard it said again and again, "The money is in the list."But there are plenty of other reasons than just this to make list-building your first step.

If you begin by building your list, you further validate how much interest there is in a certain niche. If you can't get people to join your list, then you have a much lower chance of being able to sell them a product.

With a list, you can also get feedback on what people want or test sales pages to products you have not even built yet. Countless people have spent way too much time developing products or services no one wants.

I am not suggesting you sell people something that does not exist, but you can test sales pages to see if people will click a Buy Now button (just don't take their money quite yet—that is illegal in most countries).

Another big reason for building the list first is that you can't learn, or do everything, at once.

There are many ways to build lists, but a simple squeeze page (lead capture page for collecting name and email) is perhaps one of the simplest sites to set up. (Go to www.createautomateaccelerate.com/ resources to get access to a free autoresponder and lead page builder— you can have something up in a few minutes.)

If you can't do this, then you will likely struggle for months when it comes to setting up the rest of your business. One step at a time.

Build your list and start to generate a small amount of traffic. Enough to build a small list to start the wheel rolling. Then move to the next step.

Step 2

Promote other people's products before building your own.

Why?

Again, several reasons...

Firstly, it is a way to start generating revenue quickly. Now be under no illusion; this probably won't replace your income quite yet. But it will help generate funds to re-invest.

This is much faster than developing your own product. Someone else has already done the weeks or months of hard work. Signing up to an affiliate program and adding your affiliate link to an autoresponder sequence only takes a few minutes.

Another reason that is often overlooked is it can be used to help test the potential of your niche or a specific product idea.

If you find you can sell someone else's product very well, then it may make sense to start developing your own (and therefore keep a higher percentage of the profit). If you can't, then you may want to reconsider your original plan.

A third reason is that if you do this well you can start developing a good relationship with other influencers in your niche.

If the product you are promoting is complimentary to the one you plan to make, then the product owner is more likely to listen to you when you later ask them to promote your product. (Assuming you have already done well promoting theirs.)

This can save countless hours when trying to recruit your affiliates later on. If you impress the product owner with your efforts first, then he or she will take you seriously. And if that goes well, you will have a foot in the door for reaching many more targeted affiliates through their network.

Step 3

A much longer step than the previous two, but equally valuable.

Building your own product takes time, but can be highly rewarding. (Both financially and emotionally.) But there are a few things to consider...

Firstly, start simple. Chances are you will make many mistakes, so learn to fail fast.

Remember the MVP (minimum viable product), the concept popularized in *The Lean Startup*. Basically, this is the minimum you need to create to start getting customers. Not a lot of customers, just enough to start using the product and to give you feedback (and hopefully some cash flow).

Simple does not mean low-quality (though the probability is your first efforts will be far from world-class).

There are already too many people selling complete junk, rebranded junk, or low-cost rip offs. Don't become one of them. There is no value in this and little longevity to your business.

Perhaps more importantly, there is no sense of satisfaction either. Remember, an entrepreneur is an artist, and a true artist takes pride in his or her work.

Positive customer feedback can be one of the most rewarding aspects of building a business. Negative feedback can completely ruin your day (no matter how much money you are making).

If you can't create something worth selling, then you are better off sticking to selling other people's products or teaming up with someone who can. Again, no shame in this.

Do not become a jack of all trades. Become the master in one part of your business and team up, JV, or hire everyone else.

When you build your own product, you will also need to create sales pages and set up a merchant account (a way to take payments online) and customer support. This takes time to get right, but once done, it will allow you to create passive income and scale your business.

The two big advantages to owning your own product (apart from the satisfaction) are the increased profit margins and the increased authority that comes with it.

With larger profits, you have more to invest in customer acquisition (advertising and marketing). Increased authority gives you more credibility in your niche and so improves your conversions and can help increase your influence in step two.

Finally, the combination of the larger profit margins and the increased authority means you are now ready to move to the final step...

Step 4

Time to build your own affiliate program.

If you are not yet clear, then it is important to understand that being an affiliate and having an affiliate program are polar opposites.

As an affiliate, you are sending traffic to other people's websites. Running an affiliate program means other people (other affiliates) are sending traffic to you.

The great thing about affiliate-driven traffic is that it usually comes with a recommendation attached (therefore increasing conversions and further enhancing your reputation). Even better, you only pay for what converts to a sale.

The fourth step completes the cycle and returns full circle back to step one. With the additional traffic from affiliates, you now increase your list size, and, in particular, build a buyers list. It is the buyers list that is the most valuable list of all.

With this expanded list and increased reputation, you can now increase your sales as an affiliate to other people's products. You also have more people to sell to as you build new products.

Additional products give you more traffic from affiliates. This, in turn, gives you a bigger list and the cycle continues.

If you look at virtually every Internet guru, this is the spiral growth path they follow.

It is possible to jump to step three first, but doing so will only delay revenue and cause potential problems and delays in getting your own product released.

When you understand this cycle, it will give you a much clearer idea of where you should be focusing your efforts right now. It also gives you a better perspective on where everything else fits in and how it all connects together.

If you don't understand it, then chances are you will be jumping from one step to another and delaying any end result.

Pause for thought. Ask yourself...

What other businesses or gurus do I know of that are using this process? Exactly how are they doing it?

What elements of this four-step cycle (if any) do I already have in place?

How can I use this concept to focus my current business growth efforts?

CHAPTER 16

IS YOUR POSITION GETTING PERSONAL?

"I'm not interested in people positioning me next to other artists."

– Lady Gaga

I know many Internet "experts" constantly try to teach that you should do personal branding. I think that this is often (not always) bad advice.

Choosing to position your business as a personal brand (e.g. Leon Jay) over a company brand (e.g. FusionHQ) without considering the implications can be very short-sighted.

Each has their pros and cons, and when done well, a blend of both can be achieved.

The logic I hear used again and again is that "People buy from people. This is only semi-true. More accurately people buy from people they trust. They also happen to buy from companies they trust.

Perhaps you are one of those unfortunate people who are born with an untrustworthy face. (Yes, studies have shown that this is a real thing. And no, it has no direct correlation to the reality of whether you are, or are not, actually trustworthy—only how trustworthy people perceive you to be.)

If so, then you may struggle to build a personal brand. It is not your fault. Just the luck of the genetic draw. Not to say you can't do it, just that you will need to work much harder at it.

Nor does everyone have the writing style or personality type that will do well with this approach. So many people tell me they plan to build a YouTube channel because that's where the traffic is. Yes, it is there. But over 50 percent of all the videos on YouTube get less than 500 views. Only 5 percent get over 100 thousand views, and only 1/3 of 1 percent get more than a million.

Why? Because they are boring, or the people in them are uninspiring. Not everyone was born to be a presenter, entertainer, or engaging educator. Focus on your core skills instead of trying to compensate for your weaknesses.

(Also, on a side note, even if you do get one million views, this only amounts to about $2,000 in ad revenues, so you better have a good business on the back end.)

But actually, this is the least of the considerations (though a consideration none the less).

The real big question is what business are you in, and what do you plan for your business's future?

If you are thinking to sell your business, then a personal brand may limit your options or reduce your sale price. If you want to pass it on to your children, you may find this, too, is difficult or even impossible.

Take for example, Tony Robbins. Only Tony is Tony. He can build up a business with his name, but it is of limited value to others. Don't get me wrong, it is still valuable. It is just that the number of people who would want to buy it, and the price he could get for it, are much less than a company brand.

As a seller of information, it is certainly easier to become a guru or industry expert under your personal name. This is especially true if your name comes with credentials (such as a Ph.D.).

While it is a valid point, it does not tell the full story...

There are many company brands that sell information and have still managed to build a loyal following. Think of WebMD, SelfGrowth. com, Nightingale-Conant (this used the founder's names, but was branded as a company), and even the Discovery Channel.

Another big advantage of a company brand is you can leverage multiple people to create and deliver content.

This combines many reputations together, gives you access to a wider audience, and allows you to tap into more networks. In addition to this, you can scale much easier, and you no longer rely on just one or two people to be the face of all the content.

In many of these examples, many personal brands are also either built, or absorbed, and enhanced as a by-product of the company brand.

For example, the majority of Nightingale-Conant's products are made by celebrities in their own right. By having the celebrity contribute a product to their range, the company's reputation is enhanced. Likewise, by having a product produced by Nightingale-Conant the celebrity's reputation and audience are expanded.

Another example is Rich Dad, Poor Dad. Initially the title of a book, Robert Kiyosaki strategically developed it into a company brand. This brand he then later sold.

How did he do it?

By publishing a series of other books by different authors under the same brand name. All the time the emphasis was on the brand, Rich Dad, Poor Dad, not on himself. However, he also built his personal brand in tandem with the company brand. A very clever move.

This made it far more valuable than if it had been Robert alone.

If you look at companies such as Apple and Virgin, they leveraged very heavily off a charismatic CEO, but in both cases, the focus remained on building the brand identity.

What about that concept that people buy from people?

Armand Morin (a highly successful Internet marketer) once told me that after he removed his name from his products, they actually sold more. By removing his face from the products and leaving only his company brand, he increased his sales.

Mark Ling (another very successful Internet business owner) told me the very same thing. In all his tests (both on software and information products), he found that a brand converted better than his personal name.

As both of these are extremely successful business owners, both generating many millions of dollars, I listen to what they have to say. Both guys do extensive testing and don't just regurgitate what they hear from others. They know what works.

And neither of them have what I would describe as an "untrustworthy face," and both had built a decent reputation in their respective niches.

Now I am not suggesting you should not build a personal brand. There are many benefits.

You have greater recognition, you have greater influence when you speak, and you can build rapport more easily than a faceless brand, and for some fame is the primary goal.

At the end of the day, in either case, you should evaluate your product, your audience, and most importantly, your goals. It is far better to be clear about your long-term strategy from day one and know exactly why you are choosing it.

Pause for thought. Ask yourself...

What company brands can I think of in my industry?

What personal brands can I think of in my industry?

What would be the advantages of a company brand in fulfilling my purpose?

What would be the advantages of a personal brand in fulfilling my purpose?

How could I combine both approaches for my project, and how would that look?

SECTION 2: AUTOMATE

"The first rule of any technology used in a business is that automation applied to an efficient operation will magnify the efficiency. The second is that automation applied to an inefficient operation will magnify the inefficiency."

– Bill Gates

CHAPTER 17

THE KEY TO FREE YOURSELF

"Besides black art, there is only automation and mechanization."

– Federico Garcia Lorca

No doubt you have heard it said, "Work on your business, not in your business." But what does this really mean, and are you doing it?

Most business owners are the lowest paid, most stressed employees in their business. The sad part is that, for the majority, this is unlikely to ever change. Yet it does not have to be that way.

For many years, I struggled as an entrepreneur. I read a lot of theory, but in retrospect, it shocks me how little I truly understood or applied. Each day I would be working to fulfill clients' requests, working to get new orders, and trying to keep my accounts in order (which was nothing short of stressful).

Then something changed. Not overnight, mind you. But it was a very definite change that began to slowly and surely take place. I started to automate and create systems for everything.

Systems are one of those words that send all but the super nerds to sleep. Yet it is systems that create order from chaos. And I can assure you chaos was the dominant experience of my working day (and night).

You will hear me repeat again and again, there are only two ways to automate anything: machines and people.

In the case of computers (machines), software creates the systems that define the automation. With people, it is SOPs (standard operating procedures) and proper training.

In the early days of your business, it will not grow itself. Nor will it plan itself and make itself run in an automated fashion. It is your job to be conscious of this goal. It is your job to ensure it happens. And it is your job to forever work in your business if you don't.

Whether you want to build an asset worth more when you sell it, a business you can pass to future generations, something that is stable even should you go on holiday or become sick, or something that you can keep growing…systems and automation are a must.

This is something that isn't optional. Either you do it or you find someone else who can. Either way, from a logistics perspective, it needs to be your company's number one underlying priority.

Every department needs this approach applying to it. From analytical departments, such as programming or accounting, to more creative departments, such as marketing or design.

It does not matter, at this point, if you are a one-man band or managing a team of thousands. The principle is the same. Use, and consistently improve, systems and automation to become more efficient.

In the following section, we will look at building our teams, tools, and systems to help you achieve this. At the end of the day, though, this is a guideline. Each business is unique and will need its own unique systems to make it run optimally.

Pause for thought. Ask yourself…

What systems do I currently have in place?

What do I wish I could automate in my business the most?

Which parts of my business would benefit the most from automation?

CHAPTER 18

THE SECRET TO CREATING TIME

"When a team outgrows individual performance and learns team confidence, excellence becomes a reality."

– Joe Paterno

The secret to creating time is simple. More people. Yes, you will need a team. No excuses.

I am bored of having this argument with beginners who think they know better or are somehow an exception to the rule.

I will be blunt… If this is you, then stop fighting the point and start actively building your team today.

I have heard every argument under the sun. "I don't work well with others," "I can't find the right people," "I can't afford to hire anyone just yet," "ONCE I am more successful, I will build my team," "I don't need one just yet," or my absolute favorite, "It's not that easy." It's not that easy!

No one said it was easy. You want easy, go back to doing first grade math puzzles, watching soap operas, or get a job flipping burgers.

You are building a business. If it were simple and required little effort, everyone would do it. The reason there is so much untapped potential is most people are too lazy to take advantage of it.

Let's look at the facts for a minute…

In his book, *Good To Great,* Jim Collins identified having "the right people on the bus" as one of the most important factors to a company having outstanding success.

No matter if it is the artist, musician, actor, sports star, or the business man, not one has achieved much of significance without a "bus full of people" supporting him or her.

Since the beginning of time, men and women have come together and worked together to achieve the seemingly impossible. Even Michelangelo had assistants to help with his amazing feats, such as painting the Sistine Chapel. He may get all the glory, but he did not do it alone.

Many famous business individuals and Internet gurus are positioned in the limelight, much as other movie, music, and sporting celebrities are. Yet, in each case, there are multiple people hiding in the shadows, who are all equally as important.

Let me ask you... Does a winning athlete get his coach, sports psychologist, masseuse, trainers, team members, managers, etc. before or after he wins the gold?

Does an actress get her agents, managers, voice coach, acting trainers, professional photo shoots, etc. before or after she wins an Oscar? And can she become famous without the other actors, film crew, directors, producers, and film distributors?

Does a musician have tutors, coaches, managers, roadies, sound engineers, producers, and other high-level band members before or after getting a number one hit?

Of course, the answer in every case is BEFORE.

Now sure, they don't all start with the best and biggest team on day one. But in every case, they are lifted to the next level of their success by the quality of the team and network that surrounds them.

And so it is with business.

In a recent report "The 18 Mistakes That Kill Startups," Paul Graham (founder of the incubator that helped start DropBox, Stripe, and Reddit) listed having only a single founder as the first mistake.

He also went on to list hiring bad programmers as another top mistake.

Now truth be told, it is not just programmers. Your entire team needs to be good, ideally the best. As Red Adair put it, "If you think it's expensive to hire a professional to do the job, wait until you hire an amateur."

Jim Collins even stated that the team was more important than the product or idea. A good team can go anywhere and achieve almost anything. A bad team is doomed to failure or mediocrity at best, even with the best ideas.

Skills can be taught, but attitude is very difficult to change. And attitude is everything.

A word of advice. If you have a team already, then evaluate it. If you have dead weight, then shed it fast. You can go much faster with a lean, efficient, and motivated team than with a large, bloated, and despondent one.

So how do you begin building a team if you don't yet have one?

Obviously money helps, but it is also not 100 percent necessary.

I will say it again—zero money it is not a good enough excuse for not starting to build a team today. Indeed, if you are broke, then you need to put together a team faster than someone with money.

Here are some of the most common options:

Partner

By partnering with others in the early days, you may not keep 100 percent of the business, but you do at least get a business. (And, as mentioned before, you actually increase your chances of success.)

However, all partners are not created equally. The wrong partnership can end in a fast track to nowhere.

Many people are attracted to other people like them. This is especially true when starting a business. The problem is we already have us; we need different people that compliment us, not duplicate us.

Your partner should bring something to the table that you don't.

If you are creative but have no eye for detail or hate systems, then perhaps you need someone that can match this imbalance. If you have marketing skills but hate tech stuff, maybe you need to find a tech guy. If you have time but no money, then maybe you need to find someone who can contribute financially.

There are many different aspects to this balancing act. However, there is one factor above all others that will seal the doom of your project if not right…

Are they too much of an entrepreneur?

Some people are; some are not. Many think they want to be, but just don't have what it takes.

In the same "18 Mistakes" report, Paul Graham also notes that the number of successful companies that are begun by people not willing to quit their day job is very few. Are you, and anyone you partner with, willing to quit your job and run on thin air for as long as it takes?

I tried to partner with a friend many years back and learned this lesson the hard way.

Things started okay, and for the first two to three months things were going well. We were turning enough of a profit to keep the business running and feed ourselves. But only just.

Just ten weeks after beginning, my partner's savings ran out. Despite having enough to live on, he started missing his creature comforts. Nice wine, expensive food, regular visits to the cinema...

My friend was a hard worker. But he was a worker, not an entrepreneur.

He had no problems working hours and hours if he knew how much he would make. But he lacked the persistence and could not cope with the uncertainty of how much we would make and how long it would take.

He is a good friend and highly talented employee. But was terrible as a business partner.

When deciding whether to partner with someone make sure you can:

- Compliment (not duplicate) each other's personality and skill sets.

- Find someone who is long-term focused.

- Trust them with everything. Without trust, you will have nothing.

- Be able to argue and challenge each other, but without taking it personally.

- Share a common purpose and vision.

Outsource

Outsourcing means different things to different people. It is important to be very clear what you mean when you use the term "outsourcing."Many people think of outsourcing as hiring people online through sites such as Elance.com and oDesk.com. And this can be an interesting way to hire people for short-term jobs or recruit long-term contractors from different countries.

The important point to remember is that big companies that are known for outsourcing (such as Microsoft or Nike, etc.) are not hiring people on oDesk. They have actual offices or factories with full-time employees and managers in place. Very different.

I hear a lot of Internet gurus shout the mantra of "Just outsource it." The truth is it can be much harder than that, and most people I know don't outsource to casual freelancers unless they have to.

There are a lot of people competing for jobs on these outsource sites. Finding the ones worth working with can be akin to finding the proverbial needle in a haystack.

A few tips…

- Only hire those with plenty of feedback and only those with a 90 percent or higher positive rating.

- Look for people who specialize in the skills you need.

- Ask candidates to submit samples of previous work.

- Interview them before hiring. Ensure they show up on time and communicate clearly.

- Never pay less than four to five dollars per hour. Even in cheap locations, you will, to some degree, get what you pay for.

- In your ad, request candidates to reply with a strange phrase in the subject line. I usually ask them to reply with the subject line "peanut sauce."

This last suggestion can save you hours of frustration. This allows you to easily filter auto submissions (many companies have auto submit scripts with canned applications). More importantly it helps you identify who can and who cannot read, comprehend, and complete a very simple task.

If they get this wrong, then the future is not likely to improve any.

Once you have found someone good, hire them full-time as soon as you can. If you don't, someone else will, and you will be back to trolling through the dross.

Most freelancers are simply looking for the best pay. Makes sense, as they have no team commitment or emotional investment in a project. If someone is skilled and can work with your team, then get them on board and working exclusively for you.

If you do work with outsourcers from a different culture (or build your team in a foreign country), then make sure you take the time to research that culture. It can save a lot of headaches and misunderstanding. For an example of this, if you have not yet done so, go watch the movie *Outsourced*.

Hire Local

Depending on where you are in the world, and what your budget is, then this may or may not make sense.

Don't make decisions based in false economy though. Often, having someone work in person with you will get things done twice as quick and will have a string of other benefits.

If you hire an outsourcer for $10/hour, you may be better hiring someone locally for $20. Never forget, it is not how much you pay, but what you get for your money.

Another option that is becoming increasing popular is to relocate yourself. As I have already explained, this is something I did myself when starting my last company.

By moving to another country, you can get the best of both worlds. Cheaper employees and the benefits working together in person. Plus your own living costs are dramatically reduced.

If you are doing things on a shoestring, this may be, by far, your best choice. (Also, it should be noted I did this together with my wife and four-year-old daughter—so be careful before making too many excuses as to why you can't.)

Commission-Only Basis

This works very well for a few positions.

Certainly sales, affiliate management, and some copywriting, marketing, or lead gen positions are all suited very well to a commission-only deal. Personally, I love this type of agreement.

If someone is very good, they will earn way more than on a salary. But that is the catch, they must be very good.

I know both many employees and employers resist this. Employees are afraid they won't make enough; employers are afraid they will pay far more than they need.

If an employee is really good and has faith in your product and in themselves, they will have no trouble with this arrangement. Many will embrace it or even demand it.

As an employer, there is the potential to have someone fill the role that you could not otherwise afford to hire. They would simply be worth too much. This type of person is invaluable to your business. There is also no risk to you, as you only pay for results.

To attract the right person, though, you will need to be generous. Being frugal here will only put off serious players and will ultimately cost you more in the long run.

Make sure that you have a good system in place to track the sales. This way you have nothing to lose and everything to gain.

Friends and Family

In short, don't hire friends and family unless it makes real business sense.

A lot of people start with friends and family because they are cheap and easy. Often, one person wants to help the other out and means well. However, so often it ends in disaster because the skill sets and personality types are not matched to the requirements.

The bottom line is, if you would not hire them as staff, or partner with them if they were not your friend or family member, then it is best not to do so out of desperation, pity, or charity. It is simply not a good start and will possibly kill both your business and your personal relationship.

Joint Venture (JV)

In this situation, you are looking for a partnership between two businesses. This allows both partners to run their own businesses and teams independently, but to collaborate together on specifically defined projects.

In this case, typically one of the partners will provide their expertise, intellectual property, or network in exchange for a royalty on each sale.

This can be another way to kick-start your ideas when starting out on a budget. I have done this many times over the years, and it has proven to be a very profitable approach with a high degree of flexibility.

You will see many large companies doing this all the time. But really, it is a strategy that is suited to businesses of any size.

That said, as with any business relationship, make sure it is a good fit before agreeing to it.

Contract Out

If the budget allows, then contracting can be another efficient way to build your team.

This is especially good if you need a professional part-time, or you lack the budget, managers, and managerial skills to hire your own team.

Examples include accounting, lawyers, graphic artists, customer support, advertising, video editing, and even programming. It is similar to hiring freelancers or outsourcing, but for this definition (far from technically accurate, but to help differentiate) you would be contracting another company to work for you, not an individual.

If you are using an agency, you will usually pay more than when hiring a private freelancer. However, it can come with some solid benefits, especially with things like programming or more complex support.

This is one of those times you need to be really careful of false economy. An agency recruits, trains, and manages the team. They also rely on maintaining their reputation.

A support agency, for example, will need to replace and retrain anyone who leaves. This can be a huge time and cost saver.

Freelance programmers are notorious for moving on and leaving you with code no one else wants to touch. An agency ensures consistency and the ability to fix things or continue development even if a specific coder leaves.

In both cases, the savings can run into the thousands and, long-term, easily offset the short-term increased cost.

Internships

Running intern program is not just for large companies. I have known even "solopreneurs" to do it.

Offering internships allows you to exchange training and work experience for free or low-cost labor. We have done this in the past and have been very surprised at the standard of people applying. Our intakes have included a world-leading e-commerce lawyer, a professional speaking coach, and a marketing director that had worked on some very big projects. (And this was for an unpaid internship.)

I would suggest, if you do go down this route, that you make sure the program lasts for at least three months. Otherwise, it can be hard to recoup the cost of training. It depends on the position and the person being hired, of course.

As we mentioned earlier, hiring a good team is not easy. Even proper recruitment agencies and PR departments suffer from poor success statistics. So don't be too hard on yourself if you don't always get it right.

I have spoken to far too many people that claimed they were never going into another partnership or hiring another person because of bad experiences.

Sorry, just because it did not work before does not give a valid excuse to not try again. See it as though you are now one step closer to finding the right people.

The truth is that successful businesses are built by teams of more than one, and more times than not, they are founded by more than one person. I would also suggest that, in the vast majority of cases, those same founders have had more failed partnerships and bad hires than the number of those that eventually made them successful.

Making mistakes and getting it wrong is normal. Having the persistence to learn from those mistakes and to keep trying until success is reached is rare.

This is one of the core reasons why so many businesses fail and so many entrepreneurs give up: a lack of persistence and inability to learn from mistakes made. Don't be one of them.

Pause for thought. Ask yourself...

Who makes up my current team right now?

What types of team members (partners, freelancers, employees, etc.) am I using now?

How would I benefit from working with a great team?

What could I do to be building a better team?

CHAPTER 19

NOT ALL TEAMS ARE CREATED EQUALLY

"The secret to successful hiring is this: look for the people who want to change the world."

– Marc Benioff, CEO of Salesforce

Did I mention, finding the right people is not easy?

I have given a few recruitment tips in the previous chapter. Here are a few more…

To recruit teams, most people will search Elance, oDesk, Fiverr, or a job recruitment board. While I have had some success with these, in my experience there are far better options.

Many of the recruits we get come through simply asking our existing networks. Programmers, for example, know other programmers. They also know who is good and who is not.

Extending this even further, social media allows us to reach many more people. Certain fan pages, social groups, or your own followers can provide a diverse range of possibilities. (This can work for almost all types of team building, from seeking a freelance contractor to a full-time employee.)

Sometimes asking is all it takes.

Another much-overlooked resource is forums. Forums exist for almost every specialist niche you can think of. Programming, artists, design, video editors, marketing, and sales.

There are many really cool reasons for using forums to recruit. To start, not so many other people do. Secondly, the people there are actively interested in a subject. Thirdly, you can see the history of posts people have made, so you can see if they are asking or answering questions, and at what level. And the icing on the cake, it is usually free to send someone a PM (private message) and ask them if they are interested in some work.

If you are looking for someone in a specific location, then Craigslist can sometimes help. As can local universities, employment agencies, or putting an ad in the local paper. Sometimes you just need to get creative.

Another of my favorites, especially for establishing partnerships, is industry-specific live events, conferences, or seminars. Attending these, both as an attendee and as a speaker has, over time, been very profitable.

There is no single source for team members. It pays, in this case, to cast your net wide, scour high and low, and be persistent.

Some additional tips:

- If someone is late or making excuses before you have even hired them, don't waste any more time. Move on quickly.

- Ask for references, and follow up on them. Some companies do not allow staff to give bad references on previous employees, but many will (or are not aware that they shouldn't). Either way, you could save yourself a lot of headache with just a quick call.

- Ask for examples of work before asking for qualifications. In my opinion, many degrees are next to worthless. I would prefer to hire a great designer based on his or her portfolio, not his or her grade. Self-taught people are extremely passionate, and many degrees are out-of-date by the time a student graduates.

- A top tip from Elon Musk... Ask people what problems they have solved in the past. If they were the ones who solved the problem, they will be able to explain how in detail. If not, they will be vague in their answer.

- Give the final candidates a test project. As Perry Marshall says, "Audition; don't interview." A real life test will tell you more than any interview.

- Always look for good attitude and willingness to work as part of a team (for most positions). If someone isn't working out but has a great attitude, look to see if you have him or her in the right role. Maybe changing the person's position could be far better than simply letting him or her go.

- Above all, don't hold on to dead weight. A negative attitude is like a disease. It will spread.

You may have heard people talking about A, B, and C players.

C players are the dead weight. No amount of time or effort is likely to change that.

Many good people are B players. They can get the job done well and will usually cause little problem. However, they are not likely to give 110 percent and can easily get dragged down in office politics or distracted by C players.

A players are the ones you want. They will give it their all. They have the perfect combination of skills and attitude. They can also lift B players up to a B+ or, in some cases, an A.

A players like to play with other A players. They want to make a difference, and they will be worth many times more than several B players put together or an entire herd of C players.

The problem is, they are hard to find, and they usually know their worth (meaning you need to cough up and pay what it takes). Being frugal with your team could be the most expensive mistake you make.

Think about Google as an example. If the founders had started by hiring programmers in developing countries, do you think they would be one of the world's most powerful companies today?

That said, growth is all about stages and constant readjustment. Don't be too hard on yourself if you don't get the best people from day one. If you build a team, you will make hiring mistakes. However, if you don't build a team, you will be making the biggest mistake of all.

And if you are sitting there reading this, thinking it does not apply to you, then stop reading now. Waste no more of your time. Go get a job this minute. Building a business is not for you. (Unless you plan to be a freelancer, which is basically still a job, just with more flexibility but less security and benefits.)

Final words on this…

In the beginning, your team will be small. Probably just two. (Two is the minimum.) In the early days, you will need to fill multiple roles. This is normal.

However, the only way you will grow is to replace yourself for every role you can, one at a time.

Do not fall into the trap of thinking, "I can do this myself" or "I can save money if I do it" or "I need the cash." This is all short-term thinking.

If you want to have a bigger business, then you need to do today what a business larger than yours already does. Then tomorrow you will have that business. Alternatively, keep doing what you are doing today, and you will still have the same business tomorrow that you have now.

Now that should be quite clear. Let's move on to mapping out and strategizing your business. First…

Pause for thought. Ask yourself…

Which positions do I really need to start recruiting for right now?

Where would I most likely find A players for each of these positions?

CHAPTER 20

MAPPING THE WAY

"Plans are nothing; planning is everything."

– Dwight D. Eisenhower

A while back, a member of my mastermind group asked me to help him figure what he needed to do next in his business. He is a very intelligent guy and had already built a large following and a solid income stream.

But he was stuck.

Five minutes later he walked out just muttering "of course!"So what happened in those few minutes?

Simple. I had him map out his business as a basic flow chart.

On it were sources of traffic, entry point pages to his business, sales pages, and his autoresponder messages. Arrows connected sources of traffic to where leads would go, what happened next, and to where people would go if they clicked on links in each of the email messages.

Next, I had him list the average numbers at each stage. How many people were coming each month from each traffic source, how many would opt in, how many would buy, and how many bought from each of his email follow ups.

From this simple diagram, he could see in seconds what needed to be done. As they say, a picture is worth a thousand words. (And in this case, thousands of dollars.)

For those without a business, this process can be even more invaluable. It identifies priorities, helps you foresee what will need to be done, helps you avoid making unnecessary mistakes, and creates both focus and a reference point for your team.

It is so easy to do, yet almost no one does it.

Having a good map of your business drawn out really helps. You can then see the flow of your business. Where are customers coming from? What is the first point of contact to your business? What is the sales flow? What is the product delivery flow? What is the post purchase or sign up flow? What is the support flow? What is the flow for creating new products or services?

By literally drawing this out on a large whiteboard or flipchart paper, you can often find areas for improvement just by seeing how things currently operate. The real magic, though, comes when you overlay your key metrics to this map (more on this later).

To help, I have included a basic outline of what your map should look like. This will, of course, vary from business to business.

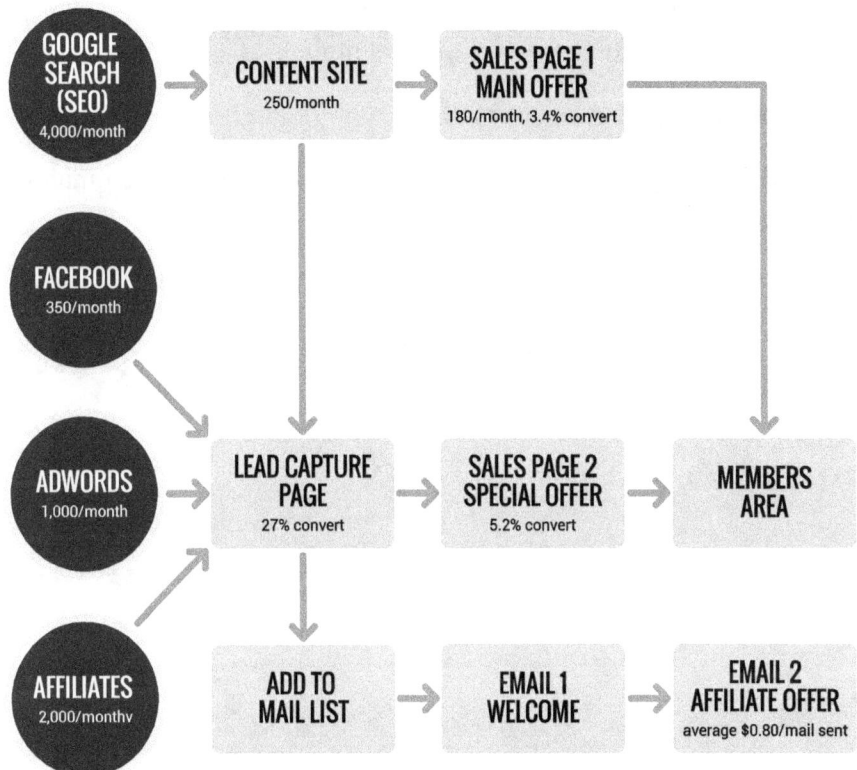

You can easily see from looking at this map any areas of weakness or potential leverage.

As you become more experienced, you can add more metrics to your map, and expand it as your business grows. Without it, mentally grasping what is going on can be overwhelming, and explaining your business flow to others near impossible.

It has been said that with clarity comes power. This process will give you the clarity and power you need to make more effective decisions and achieve better results.

Take the time now to map out your business. A basic outline will not take long, but it may well be the most important thing you do all year. Never underestimate the power of the simple.

Pause for thought. Ask yourself...

What does my business look like (or will it look like) when mapped out on paper?

What are they key metrics I can identify based on my business flow?

What could I do to improve the flow of my business to make it run more optimally?

CHAPTER 21

REALLY UNDERSTANDING LEVERAGE

"Your workforce is your most valuable asset. The knowledge and skills they have represent the fuel that drives the engine of business—and you can leverage that knowledge."

– Harvey Mackay

Leverage is one of those words used a lot. Yet it is so often empty in specifics. In this section, I want to cover a few core concepts that will help you understand where the maximum leverage is in your business.

A few years back, I wrote my first book, which received some odd objections...

My book, *Do Less Work, Make More Money,* received incredibly positive feedback—from those who read it. Many others refused to read it because they said it sounded like a scam.

Strange. These were the same people who were looking to do just what the title suggested. However, when phrased so bluntly, there was a strong negative emotional reaction.

As you know by now, I am not an advocate of becoming lazy and doing less. But I am a big believer of getting better returns on your time and creating greater efficiency and results in your life.

To help overcome these objections, and to further help people achieve just this, I developed this simple formula:

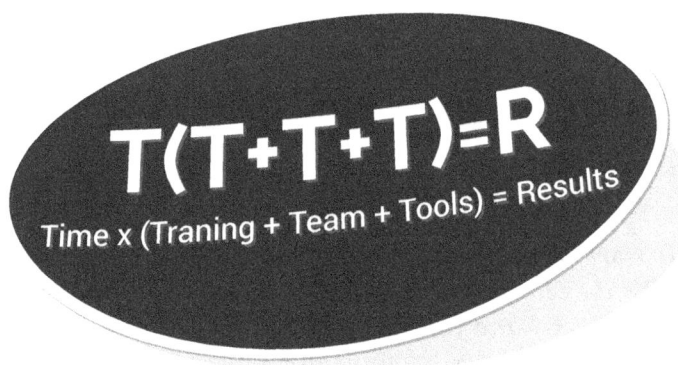

I will be the first to say it is not scientifically accurate, and there are more variables to consider. However, it illustrates very well where fast improvements can be made through more effective focus.

I should also point out that each variable can have a plus or minus effect in the equation, depending on the quality. Bad training, team, or tools can actually be the death of a business. So think quality, not just quantity.

Let's analyze this in a bit more detail, and you will see what I mean…

Time: Without time, there is no result, no matter how good every other variable. However, the more time that is given, the greater a potential net result can become.

Training: Good information will give us a much better idea of how to effectively use our time. We can learn from the mistakes, knowledge, and experience of others. Without it, we will need to make many more of our own mistakes and, therefore, take longer to get to the same end result. (If, indeed, that same level of result is ever reached.)

Team: Other people are critical to achieving large results; we have already gone into that in great detail. Remember, it is not just the size but the quality. If you have a good team and you provide them with excellent training, then they become capable of attaining better results faster.

Building your team from the right people has a massive advantage over almost all the other elements of this equation...

Each person will already have invested money and time into their training. Now if you are trying to fill that role yourself, you will need to spend money and time getting to the same stage that they are now. This means you actually save way more time than just the time a team member may spend filling any given task.

In addition to this, you also get the wisdom of each individual's past mistakes and their learned efficiency from having done those same or similar tasks in the past. In some cases, they may also bring their own tools to the job, too (for example a graphic artist may have his or her own computer and software).

When you start fully understanding the many layers of benefit and leverage a team brings, you can begin to fully grasp how foolish and ineffective it is trying to do everything yourself.

Tools: The most simple of all tools is a lever. The lever allows us to move more mass with less effort. It literally is at the root of the word leverage. At the very least, tools allow us to automate and simplify. At the other extreme, they allow us to achieve what would be impossible without them.

On the Internet, software is our number one type of tool. Yet it never ceases to amaze me the number of entrepreneurs that refuse to invest in professional tools.

Imagine a builder. In theory, he could build a house with minimal, cheap tools. But what would be the quality, how long would it take, and how long would it last?

Would you hire him? Would you back him as an investor? Would you place a bet on his success? Of course not. Yet people do this all the time when they bet on themselves as an entrepreneur and don't even buy themselves a set of professional tools.

They buy the cheap junk and then wonder why they keep getting amateur results. If you want to really grow and scale your business, think intelligently and be VERY careful of false economy.

This is not rocket science as they say. You can't expect to build a professional, lasting business with no team and inefficient tools—no matter how many training courses or coaching programs you buy.

Yet I continue to meet person after person who thinks that, by buying the next training course, they are going to discover the "missing secret." They believe success will come if only they can find the right teacher.

You can have the best teacher in the world, but unless you are prepared to invest in more than just your education, you will get nowhere. Certainly not anywhere very fast.

For the formula to be most effective, it also needs to be applied by someone with good leadership, and to a business with a meaningful purpose. Ultimately, though, it should act as a good rule of thumb for identifying where to invest your resources.

Pause for thought. Ask yourself...

How much time have I already invested? How efficient has this been so far?

What kind of team, tools, and training does my competition have access too?

What kind of team, tools, and training do most successful companies have?

What kind of team, tools, and training do I need to get the results I want?

Which areas of this formula are my business weakest in, and what can I do about it?

SECTION 3: ACCELERATE

"I really think that technology has the greatest potential to accelerate happiness of most things in the world. The companies that will ultimately do well are the companies that chase happiness. If you find a way to help people find love, or health or friendship, the dollar will chase that."

– Ashton Kutcher

CHAPTER 22

TAKING OFF

"One way to keep momentum going is to have constantly greater goals."

– Michael Korda

Getting momentum going is one thing. Continuously increasing it is another. In this final section, we will look at the aspects that make a business grow. This involves the metrics, efficiency, and enhancements to attitude.

If you have done your groundwork, the process of rapid growth will be considerably easier. If you have taken too many shortcuts, then it will be very challenging, maybe next to impossible. (Trust me, without embarrassing myself with too much detail, I have learned the hard way!)

Without a solid foundation, acceleration can do more harm than good. Many a company has crashed and burned as a result of too much success too fast. On the other hand, many more have withered and died because they failed to gain sufficient speed.

If your business is selling e-books, chances are you won't have too many problems. If you are delivering a service, selling a physical product, or developing complex software, there can be a very real problem with too many customers.

The way to manage this a little better is to calculate best- and worst-case scenarios. Research has shown that humans are not usually very good at predicting the future. Nor making an accurate estimation of the size of something, especially when they can't see it as a whole.

To help overcome this tendency of guessing in the dark, we can improve our results by thinking through the extremes...

What is the worst result that could happen in terms of sales volume? Ask yourself, what would need to happen for that result to become a reality? On the other extreme, what is the best result you could possibly expect? What would cause that to become a reality, and what would be the impact on your business systems? (That is, can you handle it?)

When you are more aware of the potential variation in results, and the associated reasons behind them, you are able to make better decisions. These better decisions will certainly not guarantee a smooth ride up, but they will help reduce the turbulence.

Things to consider include:

- Can our technology infrastructure handle the maximum potential growth?

- Will our suppliers be able to meet our demand?

- Do we have a big enough team to deliver on our promises?

- Can we scale our customer support at a sufficient rate?

- Do we have enough working capital to manage any costs to scale that fast?

- Do we have enough working capital to survive if we end up with the worst-case scenario?

Each business is going to have its own areas of potential weakness. However, they really come down to supply, staffing, support, technology, and cash flow.

Likewise, the optimal numbers for you will depend on your industry, your overheads, your margins, and your rate of growth. Learn to ask the right questions, though, and you will be way ahead of the pack in getting this right.

In the next chapter, we will look at the different metrics you can monitor that will help you grow in a balanced and optimized way.

Pause for thought. Ask yourself...

What are the best- and worst-case scenarios for our growth in the next month, next three months, next six months, next year, and next three years?

In each of these scenarios and time frames, what would need to happen for that to be a reality?

Based on these answers, what are our realistic growth goals and the time frames to achieve each?

What processes do I need to put in motion today to make this happen?

CHAPTER 23

MEASURE, MONITOR, AND MODIFY YOUR M...

"Leadership means forming a team and working toward common objectives that are tied to time, metrics, and resources."

– Russel Honore

If you go for a health check with a doctor, he or she will measure many of your body's variables to help establish your degree of health. If you go to a personal trainer, he or she will do the same to identify your level of fitness.

If you want to keep an eye on the health and fitness of your business, then you need to know its metrics. These are the variables that define how well it is doing and help identify areas of weakness.

There are three major benefits to tracking metrics…

You can set goals and measure progress. You can continually run tests to see if what you are doing is creating an improvement. And you can see areas of weakness to find out what will benefit the most from some attention.

In this chapter, we are going to focus on this last benefit.

In his theory of constraints, E. M. Goldratt points out that the maximum efficiency of a system is limited by constraints (any bottlenecks). That is to say, the weakest link will likely offer the greatest opportunity for increasing total output with the least amount of effort.

While there are some critics of his theory, the basic premise is a decent place to start evaluating where your resources are best targeted for maximum return. To do this, you need to know your numbers.

Earlier we talked about drawing the map or flow chart of your business. This is really the foundation for identifying where many of the metrics specific to your business are. It also shows you visually where you should be focusing your energy to get the fastest improvements.

The more metrics you can add to your business map, the more potential bottlenecks you can find. To help you get started, I have listed some of the metrics we measure and have given a brief explanation how to calculate them…

Company Metrics:

- **Total monthly revenue** – This is the total of all money taken in for each month.

- **Total monthly cost** – This is the total spent for each month for all outgoings.

- **Total monthly profit or loss** – This is the total revenue minus the total cost.

- **Per unit cost** – This is raw cost to supply each product or service to one customer.

- **Total number of SOPs** – This is the number of standard operational procedures in place.

Programming Metrics:

- **Number of new bugs** – Average number of bugs reported each month

- **Number of bugs fixed** – Average number of bugs fixed each week/month

- **Number of commits** – Number of times code is updated to live servers

- **Server up time** – Percentage of time the servers are online

- **Average home page load time** – Time it typically takes people to load the home page

- **Average admin area load time** – Time it typically takes people to load admin area

- **Code test coverage** – Percentage of the code that is covered by auto testing

- **Code achieved** – Total amount of code created per week (measured in complexity)

Support and Training:

- **Ticket to customer ratio** – Average number of tickets per customer

- **Customer satisfaction** – This is based on speed of response, technical accuracy, customer comprehension, and friendliness.

- **First contact response time** – Average time it takes to reply to a new ticket

- **Ticket completion time** – Average time it takes to complete and close a ticket

- **Inbound call response time** – Average time it takes to answer a customer call

- **Cancelation rate** – Total paying accounts canceled per week (as percentage and actual number)

Marketing Metrics:

- **Total number of unique subscribers** – The total individual email addresses on your combined lists

- **Total number of customers** – The number of unique buyers across all products

- **Number of customers per product** – The number of buyers for each product or service offered

- **Number of visits per page** – Total number of unique visitors to each page

- **Number of returning visitors** – Total number of people who return more than once

- **Conversion rates** – The percentage of people who buy on each of our sales pages

- **Opt in rates** – The percentage of people who join our mail lists on each sign up page

- **Email opens** – The percentage of each email sent that is opened by recipients

- **Average click through rates** – The percentage of people who click on the links inside an email

- **Average unsubscribes** – The percentage of people who unsubscribe from receiving each email

- **Number of signups per week** – The number of people who subscribe to each package weekly

- **Number of active affiliates** – The number of affiliates who sent traffic in the past thirty days

- **ROI for each marketing campaign** – The total dollars made per dollar spent for each promotion

- **Average subscriber value** – The average value for each person on each opt-in list

- **Average customer value** – The average revenue generated for each person who becomes a customer

A word on these final two metrics…

You may have heard a lot about average customer lifetime value as being one of the most important numbers you can measure. For me, this number on its own is only partly useful.

What is far better is knowing the average value of a customer, or a subscriber, over set periods of time. For example, how much is each person worth over the course of one week, two weeks, one month, three months, and then the lifetime of that customer.

The reason most often given for knowing the lifetime value of a customer is so you know how much you can spend acquiring a customer. So if a typical customer goes on to spend an average of $422, and with a 50 percent profit margin you were making $211, then the logic goes that you can afford to spend close to that acquiring a customer.

Well, yes and no.

What if that $422 of revenue typically took eighteen months to generate? Can you afford to spend $200 per customer and then wait a year and a half to get your investment back? I am guessing not.

However if you knew that, in the first two weeks, that customer was worth $34 of profit, you may consider spending a full $34 per lead with the knowledge that you will be making an additional average of $177 over the next 76 weeks.

The same is true for your free lists. How much can you afford to spend acquiring a new free sign up, and over what time period can you expect to see a return on that investment?

You also need to consider that each list, no matter if free opt-ins or a specific product customer list, will have a different value. This means you need to break down and calculate the average "time value" metric for each subscriber list and each product.

What system you use determines how complex or simple this actually is. Inside of FusionHQ, we actually do this automatically. It is easy, as all the data is centralized, so we can set algorithms to figure all of these (and many other) metrics for you so they are available at a quick glance.

If you are using most other setups, you will need to find a way to setup and measure this information. Either way, it may be the most powerful metric you can uncover in your business. It will give you a clear advantage, as you know your exact available budget for both list building and customer acquisition.

If all of this sounds incredibly boring to you, don't ignore it. Find someone else to do it. (Preferably someone that gets excited by these concepts.)

I can't teach you how to get the raw data for each of the different metrics listed above. It will be unique for each business. But once again, asking the right questions will lead you to the right answers.

Metrics are the cornerstone to understanding how to grow and scale any business. The ability to measure and make use of these numbers separates the amateurs from the professionals.

If you want to keep struggling and getting mediocre results and never knowing why, then continue to ignore your metrics. If not, then measure your metrics and modify them. The results will be pure metric magic.

Pause for thought. Ask yourself...

What metrics do I need to measure and refine in my business?

Where do I find the data needed to measure each metric?

Who is the best person to measure and monitor the metrics for my business?

CHAPTER 24

THE CRYSTAL BALL

"Never stop testing, and your advertising will never stop improving."

– David Ogilvy

O nce you know your metrics, you need to make and test changes to see if you can improve them. One test can literally turn a business from making a loss to turning a profit. I have seen it happen…

I was consulting with one client, a well-known copywriter, who had built a product for generating a passive income on the side of his copywriting business. He had his sales funnel set up and had started generating leads via Facebook advertising. So far so good.

Only problem was his ROI was 0.8%. That meant he was spending a dollar to make eighty cents. Not a sustainable business. This is the point when many people give up and complain Facebook advertising is too expensive or think they must have made the wrong product.

I asked my client to run one simple test. Increase his price point. That was it. Instantly, his new business went from losing money to making money.

Now this was not a stupid guy. Yet he had overlooked this ever so simple method of increasing profit. With a change that took no more than five to ten minutes of work, he went from negative to positive cash flow. Plus, he could now afford to spend more on advertising and generate even more leads than before.

I am not suggesting that everyone will increase their revenues by increasing their prices (though it is amazing how often this will work). However, there are many factors that can create a dramatic improvement in results.

Marketers have conducted numerous tests and have found they can increase opt-in or conversion rates by a factor of anything from 0.2 percent to over 2,000 percent from a single change. The problem is, until you test, you cannot be sure which changes are bringing you those results.

Some of the common things to test for are:

- **Price** – Lower does not always convert better. Also, try ending your prices with an odd number.

- **Headline** – If it does not grab the attention of visitors, they will be gone before they see anything else.

- **Headline color** –I have seen Some tests increase conversions by over 300 percent just by changing the headline color. Make sure headlines stand out.

- **Page text** – Your sales copy is there to sell. Keep experimenting with different styles and lengths and by emphasizing different benefits.

- **Video** – Try with and without video. Try different videos. Try auto-start versus non-auto-start. Try with or without video player controls. Try different pre-start images.

- **Graphics** – Product images, especially, really help establish perceived value. People's faces, size of images, and infographics can all increase or decrease conversions.

- **Font size** – Try different font sizing. With screen resolutions increasing, making font sizes larger often increases conversions.

- **Page color** – Different colors on websites can make a dramatic difference on conversions. Depending on the niche you are in and how long your sales page is, different colors can have a big impact.

- **Buttons** – Changing opt-in and buy now buttons can have an instant result on your page's effectiveness. Test size, text on the button, button color, and button style

There is basically no aspect of a page that will not in some way affect conversions. Sometimes the differences can be small; other times it is massive. Each page is unique, and each test is different. With practice, you can begin to make better guesses at what will work and what won't. But you will never really know until you have proven it through a proper test.

So how do you conduct a proper test?

I won't go into it in full detail here. This topic is worthy of several books on its own. There are some key points to cover…

As a rule of thumb, whenever you test, only test one thing at a time. This allows you to know which change made the difference. If you change both the headline and the headline color, for example, you won't know which factor altered conversions. The changes may have even canceled each other out. There is no way to know.

The primary method of testing is known as A/B testing. This is where half your visitors see one page, half see another. It is extremely simple and effective. You just need to make sure that the method you use to rotate the pages will display the same page again should a visitor return at a later date. If not, you could reduce the accuracy of your results.

There has been a lot of popularity recently around multivariate testing. This allows you to test multiple factors on your page at the same time.

However, I don't recommend this to most people. The reason being is you need far more visitors to make your results statistically accurate.

There are many formulas for calculating whether a result is indeed statistically accurate. These combine the number of visits, the number of conversions, and the percentage difference between the results of the different tests being run.

I find that this level of detail often overwhelms people and so they give up. Though it may be frowned upon by testing gurus and statisticians, I find simplicity more effective. It gets used and is close enough most of the time.

My general rule is this…

I want at least a thousand visits to the page I am testing. Once we reach that number, we will typically make a decision, and then start a new test.

I have found that, for the first few hundred visits, the numbers can swing dramatically. By the time you hit a thousand, it has usually settled a lot. Now, usually by this point, one of two things has happened. Either we have a clear winner, or the results are very close.

In the first case, if the result has held steady that test A is outperforming test B, there is no real benefit to me finding if this improvement is a 30 percent or a 300 percent increase. It won't change my mind on which has become my new default page. The increase is whatever the increase is, so long as it is an increase. Improving the accuracy of this test is only costing time and visitors that I could be using to run a new test.

In the second case, the numbers are very close together. So we just take the better performing page. Chances are, at this point, we have identified the better page, even if it is only a small improvement. Occasionally we may be wrong. By letting it run longer, the winning result may change. But, if so, it is unlikely to be by much.

Instead of wasting precious time fine-tuning a 0.8% increase, I would prefer to focus on running a new test that will give me a much more dramatic conversion increase.

By running many tests back to back like this, we can make much faster progress overall. Never lose sight of the fact that testing is there to increase your overall progress, and the most effective way to do this is to get the largest net result in the shortest possible time.

Being too accurate and focusing on too much detail can actually be counterproductive. (Even though for the detailed analysts it may be frustrating to take such an inaccurate big picture approach as this.)

To do all this testing, you will need to use a system that has inbuilt testing or integrate with a third-party testing service. I can't tell you which is best, as it will be dependent on the amount of traffic you are getting, what you want to test for, and the platform you have built your business on.

Have clarity on what you want to achieve, ask the right questions, have the right people on your team, and it is not that difficult. If you lack clarity, hate numbers, and are trying to do everything alone, then you are going to struggle. If you are feeling, by this chapter, chances are you can tell which of these scenarios you are currently in.

It is important to know that testing is not only relevant to sales pages. It can be applied throughout your business.

Many of the metrics we looked at in the last chapter can be tested. Test different sources of traffic, product usability, changes to your services, managerial approaches, and company policy changes. You may not be able to do A/B split tests on most of these, but you can measure changes through your metric measurements.

The bottom line is this… If you want to accelerate your business growth, then measuring metrics and constantly testing them is the key.

Pause for thought. Ask yourself…

What tests can I start running today that could make a significant difference to my bottom line?

Which software is best for us to run and monitor our tests?

Do I need to find someone else to run the testing for me? If so, who?

CHAPTER 25

THE ONLY THREE WAYS TO INCREASE PROFIT IN ANY BUSINESS

"You can't have a healthy society unless you have healthy companies that are making a profit, that are employing people and that are growing."

– Michael Porter

There are, of course, many ways to make more money for your business. However, they all fall into one of three categories.

When you fully understand this concept, you can begin to consciously and consistently apply it to get very powerful results.

This idea is based on the original teaching from Jay Abraham that taught that the only three ways to grow a business are to:

1. Increase the number of clients; turn more new prospects into paying customers.

2. Increase the average transaction; get each client to buy more at each purchase.

3. Increase the frequency that the average client buys from you; get each customer to buy from you more often.

From an increasing revenue perspective, I would say he is right on the money (excuse the pun).

However, if you wish to increase profit, I offer the following modification:

1. Increase the number of sales (either by getting more new customers or getting existing customers to buy again).

2. Increase the amount of profit made from each transaction.

3. Reduce unnecessary expenses.

Let's take a look at each of these in more detail and get some ideas on how each may be achieved...

Increase Number of Sales

The number of sales is usually a baseline for most businesses for measuring their evolving success. Most people think this is achieved by driving more prospects to a sales process, but actually there are many ways we can achieve the same effective result.

1. Running split tests on your sales pages or sales processes is perhaps the fastest and simplest way to increase conversions. By steadily and systematically improving your conversion rates, you can easily double, triple, or quadruple your sales without increasing your average number of leads. You can test anything, but for fast results, try headlines, product images, page layout, product description, and price.

2. You can also increase conversions by improving your presell process. This can be done by better education or desire-building in your marketing and advertising. Another way is to establish yourself more as an authority (people trust and like to buy from experts).

3. You can capture leads from your website and then use an autoresponder to follow up with them. Most people who visit your website will never return unless they are given reason to. By

creating an automated email sequence, you can put the process of following up with a prospect on autopilot. (www.sendfish. net is a free service designed so you can do just this.)

4. Encourage customers to buy again. This will, of course, depend on what product or products you have to sell. Don't forget, though, the first sale is the most expensive sale (due to the acquisition cost), so it is well worth having a product or service you can sell again and again, or at least a range of niche-related products to generate more sales.

5. Have a system in place that encourages new customers (and even prospects who have not yet bought) to refer their friends or family. By getting your list to share your offer, you generate new leads for free (or almost free, depending on your method), and they often come with a trusted endorsement that helps increase conversions.

6. Create an affiliate program and give commissions to those who send you customers. The great thing about an affiliate program is you only pay for results, and you can always set the cost to be lower than the frontend sale price. This makes it a very low-risk lead generation strategy.

7. Integrate to other people's sales processes. This is really the most effective form of affiliate marketing. You can do this by finding another business that has a complementary and non-competing product or service, and then having them combine it with yours. The best example of this was Microsoft adding Windows to each PC sold.

8. Run evergreen promotions. These can dramatically increase your average number of sales. By following up with new prospects and/or customers and creating an automated, special, limited-time offer, you can easily increase your sales volume.

9. Sell a recurring product, service, or membership. Food, cosmetic, hygiene, and supplement companies have long benefited from having products that need to be bought again and again. If you are able to sell any of these, or a service, software, or membership access on a subscription plan, then you can put those repeat sales on autopilot.

10. Use a sales funnel to offer additional items immediately after your customer just bought. There have been studies to show that, with every passing minute after a buyer just purchased, his or her chances of buying anything else decreases. If someone just bought something, you know two important things. Firstly, they have a strong enough interest in what you are offering and trust you enough to spend money. Secondly, they have their wallet in their hand and are in a buying state. Online businesses have been taking advantage of this opportunity for years. It is pure gold—make the most of it.

Increase the Profit per Sale

Another very simple way to increase your company profits is to increase the amount of money made with each transaction. This may sound obvious, but so few people make a conscious effort to optimize this critical part of their business.

There are a surprising number of ways this can be achieved. Here are just a few:

1. Increase the price. Simple but often effective. Customers are often happy to pay more if you simply ask for more. The key here is that you should not overcharge for the sake of overcharging, but many business owners lack the confidence to ask for what their product is really worth. Sometimes increasing the price will actually increase sales, too, as the perceived quality goes up. This can be further helped by better packaging, cover,

or site design.

2. Create bundled offers. This is something Amazon.com is famous for. By grouping together products that customers typically buy together, or multiple books by the same author, they can increase the value of a transaction. If you have more than one product or service, see if you can bundle them and provide a small discount to encourage larger sales.

3. Upsell and cross-sell. This is really a slight twist on the previous idea and the sales funnel idea in the last section... First, allow your customer to make a decision and place the order. Before they check out, though, offer them something else they may want that is directly related to their initial order. Think of McDonald's for the classic example here. "Would you like fries with that?" Many computer companies do this very well, too. Upgrade your processor or memory, add a mouse or printer, or offer an extended warranty.

4. Increase your profit margins by reducing the cost (but without reducing the quality). Amazon did this with books by creating the Kindle. By delivering books electronically, they could remove the cost of printing, warehousing, handling, and shipping. Many buyers (myself included) now prefer digital books over the physical versions. Many products or services can be provided online, often making profit margins close to 100 percent. In other cases, you may simply be able to negotiate better wholesale rates or find other creative ways to reduce your raw cost and increase your profit.

5. Reduce the cost of accepting payments. Accepting credit cards is never free, and usually, neither is the payment gateway service you use to accept those credit cards. When you start out, research which provider is offering the best rates. Companies like PayPal and Stripe are not the cheapest, but they are often

competitive. What you may not realize is that, as your business grows, you can almost always get these rates reduced—but rarely will it happen without you asking. Make sure you revisit these costs every time you have significant growth in your business, and you may well save yourself some money.

Reduce Your Operation Costs

Every business comes with overheads. These are the fixed costs, most of which are only marginally proportional to your sales volume.

Things like servers, your ISP, electricity, water, rent, staffing salaries, the software you use, and other costs of doing business. Each one adds up and eats away at your bottom line profit.

The longer you have been in business, the greater the chance you are paying more than you need. Even when starting out, though, a little thought or research can save you more than you may realize.

The trick is reducing these overheads without compromising the quality of your product or service. The idea is not to be stingy or short-sighted here. But neither should you throw money away for no additional benefit.

Some suggestions:

1. Avoid expensive office rent unless you really need it. Home offices suit some people, but many will be more productive away from home distractions or will need the space to put their team. However, basing yourself in a prestigious location has no real benefit if your customers never come to see you. As discussed earlier, you may even consider moving to a different country to base your office. In Thailand, when we started, we were renting a four-story building for $500/month.

2. If you run your business online, then keep an eye on the latest

service provider's costs. For example, we just restructured our servers and saved a few thousand dollars every month. Not only that, but we actually got a much better service, too. Technology and pricing move fast, and many companies are left with out-dated systems and pricing plans.

3. Increase team efficiency. If you are paying for a team, then they are costing money. The more efficient they are, the less they are effectively costing you per task completed. There are whole books on this subject, which I highly recommend you study. One very powerful way to do this is to ensure they are using the best tools for the job (see the chapter on leverage).

4. Consolidate costs. If you are using many services that can be combined into one provider, often there is a cost-savings and a time-savings (which is effectively another efficiency cost sav-ings). For example, my company www.FusionHQ.com, along with others in this industry, provide a range of services that previously required multiple providers. We offer website build-ers, sales page builders, membership site management, autore-sponders, affiliate tracking, popup scripts, a CDN, and cloud hosting all in one dashboard. This type of consolidation can offer massive savings to anyone currently paying for multiple service providers.

5. Create a discipline of good economic practice within your working environment. Turn off equipment that is not being used, encourage staff to be more careful about wastage, and use LED bulbs. There are plenty of good websites and resources that can give you tips for better energy management. Great for the environment and your bottom line.

6. Seek good tax advice. Many business are giving money away when they really don't need to. I am not advocating tax evasion, but with the right advice, you could be saving a considerable

amount of money. Either through restructuring your business to a different jurisdiction of incorporation or simply by claiming more of your expenses. Be warned; free advice in this area may end up being some of the most expensive advice you ever take. So don't listen to me; go ask a real expert that knows your local laws and is an expert in working with your type of business.

For each of these three ways to increase profit, there are almost endless possibilities, and each will be dependent on your business, skills, team, budget, and circumstances.

I cannot possibly claim to know what you should do or even where you should start. This would be irresponsible without properly analyzing your current situation. What I can tell you, though, is your business will benefit greatly by consciously working on and improving all three areas on an ongoing basis.

For the last point, reducing expenses, you may not need to spend more than an hour or a day each month, or even once a quarter, to see what you can do to reduce costs. This will depend on your business size and speed of growth.

A great way to get ideas to focus on is to ask your team. Encourage and even reward them to submit suggestions for improvement. Educate them on the three ways to increase profit and have them look for ways you can improve each.

Often, team members see things that we can't. In *Switch*, Dan and Chip Heath highlight one extreme case in which an employee's idea saved the company around $1 billion. The suggestion was simple: buy all of their supplies from the same supplier for all their factories and negotiate better rates for bulk purchasing.

It started with the realization that the company was buying many types of gloves for the same basic purpose. This was costing the company a small fortune without them even realizing. They started to consolidate their glove purchasing to a single supplier and made immediate savings. Once they scaled this philosophy across the entire organization, the savings added up very quickly, indeed.

The probability is you don't have thousands of employees or the possibility of saving $1 billion. But even small business of just two or three people can benefit from this approach. As a business owner, you are often buried in your own tasks. Team members typically assume you can already see what is obvious to them, so they don't say anything. Ensure your team understand their contributions, ideas and suggestions are both expected and appreciated.

As for increasing customers and increasing profit per transaction, these should be a weekly objective. I spent years realizing I was focused 95 percent of the time on product development. I was giving no real attention to increasing profit.

This may sound absurd. Yet it is a far more common problem than you may realize. When you are passionate about your product and focused on what you enjoy doing, it is easy to forget the basics.

If you don't have a team whose sole responsibility it is to generate more sales and increase profits, then I suggest creating a new weekly habit...

Monday morning sit down and ask yourself "As a business, what else could we be doing this week to get more customers and to increase the profit per transaction?"

By regularly focusing on this key question, you will create a flood of ideas. Not all will be good or even possible. However, write them down. One idea leads to another, and that may be the one that will exponentially grow your business.

In chapter twenty-eight, we will look at how we can manage these ideas and decide where we should be focusing our energy.

When brainstorming this question, I recommend getting a few key members of your team together or, at the very least, grabbing a friend to brainstorm with you. Brainstorming is almost always more effective when done with at least one other person.

Pause for thought. Ask yourself...

Which ways can we reduce our operational costs without affecting quality?

Which ways could we generate more customers?

How can we increase the average amount customers spend with each transaction?

Which ways could we get customers to buy again?

CHAPTER 26

STOP, LOOK AND LISTEN

"Your most unhappy customers are your greatest source of learning."

– Bill Gates

Sometimes we are just too close to our own business to see where our biggest opportunities for improvement are. I have never met anyone who enjoys admitting that their product or service has flaws. But unless you are willing to at least face the reality that there will always be room for improvement, then it is hard to make real progress.

One of the best sources of feedback comes from actual customers. All too often we try to get feedback from friends or family, h often sugar coat reality. Paying customers are far less likely to hold back on their real feelings.

The challenge is to listen to feedback and not do one of two things: either become deeply depressed or end up in a panic trying to please everyone.

It is easy to take criticism personally, and it can be hard not to.

Learning to deal with negative comments and occasional hate mail (yes, you will get people who are nothing short of abusive) is not easy. But if you want to enjoy life and grow your business at a decent rate, you will have to.

A couple of tips here are to learn to meditate. It makes a huge difference. The second is to get a customer support team as quickly as possible. They can then filter the messages, delete the crazies that may dampen your day, and rephrase the rest into constructive feedback.

I am only human. Even with regular meditation and a philosophical outlook on life, I can still have my day tarnished by a hurtful support ticket. I can have a hundred positive comments, but it only takes one nasty comment to throw my day.

In the early stages of a business, it may be possible to try to keep everyone happy. But this does not mean you should. As you grow, this becomes impossible even if you wanted to.

You need to learn to identify which suggestions are critical fixes, which are amazing ideas, which are nice haves when you get time, and which are just a waste of time.

At FusionHQ, we listen to every customer. Each suggested feature, improvement, or fix is documented and then analyzed for its level of complexity and its potential benefit to our platform.

We also work very closely with our VIP customers. These are the guys that we know are long-term loyal customers and are making good use of our platform. We maintain personal contact with this group of customers because we know their feedback is extremely valuable.

They know the product better than most, and they are using it to generate decent incomes. Therefore, we can trust they know what they are doing, and their feedback is priceless.

We even created a live event to meet our customers in person. Each year for the past five years we have had customers fly in from around the world to train with us. During that time, we make sure our entire team, including managers, support, designers, and programmers, talk to and help actual customers.

This gives every person a much better idea of how people are using our software, what is working, where people are getting stuck, or suggestions for making it even better. Some of our best features have come as a direct result of listening.

By keeping customers happy, building momentum becomes much easier.

I suggest you take the time to stop and listen to your customer feedback. As Bill Gates points out, it can be your greatest source of learning.

Pause for thought. Ask yourself...

What are my customers saying? What are they asking for? What can I learn from this?

CHAPTER 27

GOING BEYOND THE 80/20

"The effectiveness of work increases according to geometric progression if there are no interruptions."

– Andre Maurois

I am sure by now you have heard of Pareto's 80/20 principle. It can be applied to almost any area of life, but when applied to business, it usually comes down to the following:

- 80 percent of sales come from 20 percent of your customers.

- 20 percent of your effort will net 80 percent of the result.

- 80 percent of your leads will come from 20 percent of your advertising.

- 80 percent of your business will be driven by the top 20 percent of your sales team or affiliates.

- 80 percent of your profit will come from 20 percent of your products.

The list goes on.

And why is this important?

Because if you can identify the 20 percent that is getting you 80 percent of the result, then you know where to better focus your energy.

Now here comes the really interesting part...

What happens if you expand the 20 percent to become 100 percent? Well, your results will grow of course. But more importantly, the 80/20 rule will still apply.

Yup, even though you are now focusing on the 20 percent that was making 80 percent of the difference before, now 80 percent of your new result will still be driven by 20 percent of your current efforts.

Crazy huh?

Perry Marshall went into this in great detail and explains it far better than me in his book, *80/20 Sales and Marketing*. If you have not yet read this book, then be sure to make it your next read.

In it, he talks about the 4/64 principle. That is the concept that:

- 64 percent of sales come from 4 percent of your customers.

- 20 percent of your effort will net 64 percent of the result.

- 64 percent of your leads will come from 4 percent of your advertising.

- 64 percent of your business will be driven by the top 4 percent of your sales team.

- 64 percent of your profit will come from 4 percent of your products.

If you have not figured out why yet, let me explain...

If you take 80 percent of 80 percent you end up with 64 percent. If you take 20 percent of 20 percent, you end up with 4 percent.

That means, when you apply the 80/20 rule to the 80/20 rule, you end up with a 64/4 rule.

It is possible to go even further and keep applying this to come up with a 54/0.8 rule (that 0.8 percent of your effort will deliver 54 percent of your result) and so on. But for me, the 4/64 is a more practical level to focus on.

(In his book, Perry goes on to give some excellent examples on how this plays out in many areas of life and across companies. He also developed a power curve that helps you apply this rule in a useful way. I repeat; if you have not read his book yet, then do so next.)

Now, how do you use this principle practically?

The truth is it is a lot easier to identify which affiliates HAVE driven 80 percent of your affiliate sales. It is much easier to look back in retrospect and identify which of your advertising DID drive the bulk of your sales. However it is much harder to predict the future.

That said, we can use this theory to help us strategize more effectively. By being conscious of the rule, we can both analyze any data we have from past results to help predict the future, and we can use common sense to help answer the right questions:

- Which are the 4 percent of actions that are most likely to net me a 64 percent improvement in my affiliate sales?

- Which are the 4 percent of actions my support team could take to increase support effectiveness or efficiency by 64 percent?

- Which are the 4 percent of marketing efforts I could take that would grow my leads by 64 percent?

- Which 4 percent of things could we improve in our software to increase overall quality or customer satisfaction by 64 percent?

- What is the 4 percent of things in the business we could change to reduce unnecessary costs by 64 percent?

You see, you can apply this approach to all areas of your business.

By becoming aware of this principle and learning to ask the right questions, you can speed the growth of your business exponentially.

Don't forget to train your team, too. This is an easy concept that can be taught to all members of your team, so they, too, can apply the principle in their daily routine.

Pause for thought. Ask yourself…

What areas of my business can benefit most from applying the 64/4 principle?

Which of my tasks today are 64/4 principle tasks?

How can I teach this concept to my entire team to improve their effectiveness?

CHAPTER 28

OPTIMIZING EFFICIENCY AND INCREASING EFFECTIVENESS

"Efficiency is doing things right; effectiveness is doing the right things."

– Peter Drucker

I suggest learning to optimize your time. Something that I can assure you does not come naturally to me.

I have tried many different strategies to improve my focus, make my time more efficient, and to get more done. Just about every one of the tools, apps, or strategies I have tried failed to deliver. No doubt many of them work great for other people, just not me.

If, like me, you struggle to make anything work for you, then I urge you not to give up. Finding strategies and tools that do make you more efficient is well worth the effort.

Time is our most precious resource. Indeed, the entire purpose of this book is to encourage you to use it wisely and in a meaningful way.

In this chapter, I will share with you a collection of strategies that have worked for me. These are the things that have made the biggest difference to how much I can accomplish.

The first I will only mention briefly. That is learning to delegate. This can only be done by building a team, and we have spoken enough about this already. You can only actually "create" more time by increasing the number of people doing the work. One person working for one hour is one hour. Five people working for one hour is five hours. More people equal more time. Optimizing that time is a different story.

Zero Inbox Policy

One of the simplest strategies I use is one I call my "Zero Inbox Policy." This is the discipline of keeping my inbox empty virtually all the time. I have heard every argument under the sun as to why this cannot work for other people, but in every case I promise it can be done. It does work, and you quickly get a return on the initial effort.

Every single person I have taught this to who has followed these instructions to the letter have increased their productivity, and feel great for it. (Did you know when you have an empty inbox in the Gmail app, there is a smiling sun with the message "You have no mail. Please enjoy your day!")

There are several steps to getting a good result:

1. Delete or archive everything in your inbox now, unless you need to reply or action it. Without exception, it should be deleted or hidden from view. Gmail especially has an excellent search function, so don't worry, you can always find it again if it is just archived. No need for complex folder structures. Just archive or delete. Keep it simple.

2. Unsubscribe from every newsletter or mailing list you are on unless it is really useful. Let's be honest; most are not. From marketers and local businesses to hotels and airlines, we are bombarded by mail. Create the discipline of clicking unsubscribe every time you get a chance. This helps stop future clutter and wasted time—those seconds compound and add up fast.

3. Setup auto archive rules for those emails you want to keep but

don't need to read. Things such as bank statements or PayPal "payment received" notifications. It does not take long to setup, and you will soon get a return on your time investment.

4. When you do receive a mail, ask yourself these questions in the following order: Can I delete it or archive it without doing anything else? (If so, do it.) Can I delegate this email? (If so, do it.) Can I reply with a quick one or two line reply? (If so, do it.) Do I have the time to reply properly or action the request now? (If so, do it.) If not, it gets left in your inbox until you can.

For this last step, you may also consider using an app such as Outlook that will allow you to archive a message until a set time in the future. It will then automatically return it to you, thus reminding you it still needs your attention. Great for keeping your inbox even cleaner.

Why is this process so effective?

By removing everything that you don't need, you can rapidly see what is left for you to action. It makes for a very effective to-do list. You are not overwhelmed, and it becomes very difficult for mail to "get lost." If someone in your team is waiting for a reply, then they are never kept waiting long, so things keep moving at an optimal speed.

The first time I did this I thought my email was broken. My morning email routine went from well over half an hour to less than five minutes. I have never looked back. More than seven years later, I am still maintaining my zero inbox policy.

Eliminate Time Wasters

The next strategy may seem a little radical to many, but it is one of the most effective things you can do for reclaiming more of your life ... Throw away your TV. Stop watching or reading the news. Limit social media to no more than ten minutes a day. These are all the things that occupy most people's lives when they are not working, eating, or sleeping. These activities essentially consume the majority of people's free time.

Ironic, as so many people are trying to work to make more free time. But when you die, will your last thoughts be "I wish I checked Facebook more often" or "I wish I had time to watch more TV?" I doubt it. So do something about it while you still can, and don't waste any more time than is needed.

Look, I am not saying you can't relax and enjoy a movie or keep in touch with friends or family. But checking every meaningless update, watching endless soaps, staring at advertising, or watching the news is unlikely to bring much value to anyone—least of all yourself.

News, in particular, is one of those things many people trick themselves into believing is useful. You are not keeping abreast the world by watching the news. You are being spoon fed a biased view of a tiny selection of handpicked topics that have been designed to shock and grab your attention. All of which will have become nothing but a distant memory a couple days or weeks later.

If something is truly affecting your life, you can be sure you will hear about it without having to watch the news. In short, stop watching it, unsubscribe from every news feed (unless it is industry specific and relevant, useful information), stop buying newspapers, and start filling your mind with more positive and useful information.

To-Do Lists

The next strategy is to use to-do lists. Good old -fashioned handwritten ones work best for me.

The trick here is to use three lists. One is the "big" list. These are all your ideas and things that should be done at some point. The next is your week's list. This is a selection of the items from your big list that you have identified as 64/4 principles for the coming week and anything else that just needs to get done that week.

Your final list is your "today's" list. This should be made by again applying the 64/4 principle to your weekly list and identifying those urgent things that need to get done that day.

The idea for both the weekly lists and daily lists are to write down only what can reasonably be achieved within that time frame. If you can't complete it, then it rolls over to the next day or next week.

By chunking things down like this, it helps prevent you from going into overwhelm paralysis. This is the state where you have so much to do you don't know where to begin. (Don't worry—it's not just you.)

By writing at least your daily list by hand, you get the satisfaction of crossing each item off as you complete it. This helps create the feeling of accomplishment. This is very important in keeping enthusiasm up over long periods of time.

Meditate

Another "trick" is to meditate daily. This helps clear the mind, so you can see what needs to get done, and get insights that you may not have had while in the middle of chaos. It also helps balance your emotions (which improves the quality of your decisions). It increases your ability to focus, and finally, it improves sleep, therefore giving you more energy and a clearer mind when you do work.

I used to make excuses all the time that I did not have time to meditate. If you, too, are one of those people, I can assure you that you will be one of the people who will benefit the most from this technique. A calm mind, the ability to cope with stress, and the ability to better manage time are all a result of meditation—not a pre-requisite to doing it "correctly."

If you have tried meditation before but "failed"—then you are normal.

Meditation is not about a specific feeling or ability. It is simply about having the discipline to turn up to practice each day for a minimum set period of time (for me, twenty minutes or more).

There is plenty of information online. It matters less which technique you choose that it does actually choosing one and sticking with it. Try it for thirty days, and you will see what I mean.

Systems and Automation

The next is more a business philosophy to be adopted in all you do. Look for ways to systematize and automate everything. Auto archiving email is one example we have already mentioned. With ever improving machines and software, more and more of our lives can be automated. With quality teams and good processes, a lot more can be systematized.

This is the philosophy behind the success of every franchise chain. It may seem obvious and common sense, but as they say…common sense is not all that common. Despite my understanding of this, I still need to force myself to be conscious of it and seek opportunities to keep improving this side of my business on a regular basis.

The last strategy may seem a little funny, but it is perhaps one of the things that has had the most dramatic effect of all…

Consider Death

Invest a little of your time reflecting on just how limited time is as a resource. It may just help you to deepen your level of appreciation for making the best use of it. Waiting until tomorrow is a fine line between patience and a fool's folly. Each day that passes is time you will NEVER get back. Have gratitude for each passing moment and use it well.

As the saying goes, "Treat each day as though it is your last. One day you will be right." Keeping a daily awareness of this will help you to use your time more wisely.

Pause for thought. Ask yourself...

What can I let go of in my daily routine that is not serving any real purpose?

How can I find more time to focus on what really matters?

Which strategies am I going to adopt to increase my efficiency?

CHAPTER 29

BEWARE OF THE DISEASE

"I attribute my success to this - I never gave or took any excuse."

– Florence Nightingale

There is a disease that the majority of the population carries. It is something that I am sure we all suffer from at some point in our life.

This disease, if not treated, can ruin companies. It certainly prevents each sufferer from living an optimal and fulfilling life. If it sets in too deeply, it can cause paralysis. And for companies, it can become fatal.

What is this disease?

Blame.

The word itself says it all. When you blame someone or something, you choose to b-lame. When you be-lame, you effectively cripple yourself. You are passing responsibility outside of yourself. I believe it was Wayne Dyer who taught that responsibility is the ability to respond. Effectively, responsibility is the total opposite of being lame.

As an individual, blame can be annoying and reduce the quality of your life experience. Professionally, it will severely stunt the growth of your business or, if extreme, could lead to its death. This may sound melodramatic, but history is littered with company corpses from this exact cause.

Owners, CEOs, executives, and teams throughout time have blamed external circumstances, and then, feeling powerless, they have failed to adapt. They have blamed market conditions, the economy, competitors, supply chains, customers, other team members, and even the government.

To put it bluntly, shit happens. Sometimes perhaps something could have been done to prevent it. Other times, it is beyond our control. Either way, blaming does not help.

Something may not be your fault. But it can be your responsibility. Responsibility to find a solution, adjust your course, or find a way to ride the wave until the storm passes.

I have yet to read a success story that was not rife with challenges, obstacles, and struggle. In each of these cases, the leaders did not blame and say a situation was beyond their control. Neither did they stick their head in the sand and pretend a problem did not exist. They took responsibility and regained control by finding and implementing a creative solution.

Excuses are the symptoms of blame. Apathy and non-action the result.

I don't know your personal situation, and I don't know what problems you are currently faced with. But I can almost guarantee someone else has overcome the same challenges in the past.

Personally, I escaped a life of heavy drug use and started with no money, only a high school education, a baby daughter, living in a new country where I had no contacts and lacked any idea what I was going to do. I consider myself lucky; others have had to overcome far more serious situations.

However, there is one thing in common with every one of us that have managed to overcome adversity. We did not allow anything in the external world to be excuse enough to stop us. We learned to keep blame in check and take responsibility.

If you want to accelerate your business and your life, then learn to diagnose the disease of blame in yourself and in your team. Once identified, the cure is simple. Apply a sufficient dose of responsibility and teach others to do the same.

Many years ago, I attended a business seminar in which the founder of one of New Zealand's largest car tire chains was presenting. He shared how he has taken a single store to become a chain spreading the length of the country. The key…teaching his staff to take more responsibility.

In the first few years of business, he would sit in his office, and staff would come to see him with various problems. He was not a blamer himself; he was "mister fix it." He would find solutions, and the business kept running. The problem was it could not accelerate at the pace he wanted.

He decided to run an experiment. His plan was to train his team to take greater responsibility.

Shortly after, one of his team walked in. "We have a problem…" the team member started. He cut the employee off and told him to go away until he had found a solution. A while later, the employee came back. "Okay, I found the solution. We need to…" He cut the employee off again. "If you have a solution, then go implement it."He explained that, over the course of the next month or so, the regular "problem visits" to his office became less and less frequent until they all but vanished. Instead of collapsing from an overload of mistakes, his business continued to grow. His time was freed up, and he was able to focus on expansion.

Create a company culture where blame and excuses are not indulged and where responsibility and action are rewarded. If you do this, you will feel more empowered; your team will be more empowered; and you will dramatically increase your business growth.

Pause for thought. Ask yourself...

What are my current excuses for not achieving the success or results I want?

What can I do to overcome these excuses?

How can I teach others in my company to do the same?

CHAPTER 30

I AM LUCKY, BUT NOT BY CHANCE

"Diligence is the mother of good luck."

– Sixteenth Century Proverb

People often tell me I am lucky. And I agree. Just probably not for the same reasons most people think.

The lifestyle I live is a result of many fortuitous meetings, unforeseen opportunities and some extremely lucky breaks. But it is not by accident.

It is not by chance that I decided to build my business on the Internet. It is not by chance that the business is built in such a way that it runs without me. It is not by chance that we created a recurring revenue stream.

I do not believe that most people are so uneducated they don't intellectually know that their past decisions and actions contribute enormously to their current circumstances. Yet so few people are actively planning what they want or ensuring their current actions reflect their goals.

If you want to build a successful business, you may lack the experience or knowledge to do so. But that does not mean you cannot do it.

Pretend for a moment you have gone back in time. There is no GPS, no Google maps, and even paper maps are sketchy at best. There is just you and your horse…

You have decided to visit a new city that is a few hundred miles away. You have never been there before and have only heard basic directions from a couple of people who passed through there long ago. Do you think can find your way?

Of course.

Without knowing each section of the route or what lies behind each corner, you would be able to make it. You may need to stop and evaluate your progress. You may face surprises and have to navigate around unforeseen obstacles. You may need to regularly stop and ask for directions or course correct after getting lost. But get there you can.

Some days you may be lucky. You may get excellent directions, meet the right people at the right time, and be offered food and accommodation to help you along your way.

Other days will be harder. Bad weather, misguided directions, inability to find help, or your horse being sick may slow you down.

Once you reach your destination, others may say you are lucky to have traveled so far and seen so much. Was it by luck? Yes, luck will have played its part (both good and bad). But it was not by chance.

John C. Maxwell points out that "You will never change your life until you change something you do daily. The secret to success is found in your daily routine."By having a clear goal and making steady progress each day, no matter whether you experience a "lucky" or "unlucky" day, you are far more likely to get to your destination.

I will not lie to you. There are no guarantees of success. Your goal may never be achieved. There are plenty of people who spent their lives trying and never succeeding. Some people are just far too ahead of their time to make their dreams a reality.

But there is one guarantee. If you don't try, you will never know. If you give up easily, you are pretty much guaranteed not to succeed.

The probability is that your path will be filled with obstacles you failed to predict. Knowing and planning for this is important. It helps us cope when those challenges arise and increases our odds of overcoming them.

There is such a thing as too much positive thinking. An increasing body of evidence now shows how being overly optimistic without having a healthy dose of realism can lead to failure.

Balancing the two is never easy.

You must have belief. A strong belief creates faith in what you are doing. Many religious people have claimed that it is their faith that has carried them through troubling times. You don't need to be religious, however, to have faith in your project.

It is perhaps this belief in your purpose that is the final test to see if you are on the right path. If you have such belief and faith in what you are doing that you are prepared to endure the challenges ahead, then congratulations. You have found your path.

You can make money doing something you hate or something you have little feeling for. Or you can do something that fills each day with purpose. The choice is yours and yours alone to make.

For those who are currently making good money doing something that is less than awesome, that lacks purpose and passion, I hope you have the strength to break free from the trap you have created for yourself. It is not easy, but it is possible.

Never forget…time is your most precious resource, and the ability to contribute is your greatest gift. Make the most of both.

I wish you the best of luck on your journey to creating greatness…

CHAPTER 31

AFTERWORD - FINAL THOUGHTS, CLARIFI-CATION AND A WORD OF ADVICE...

"The real metric of success isn't the size of your bank account. It's the number of lives in whom you might be able to make a positive difference."

– Naveen Jain

A note to those who missed the point and to the critics…

Since writing this book, there has been some initial feedback that asks "What about the advice given in some books that you should not follow your passion. They make a good argument that passion in business is bad."It is a good question, and I think it is a lack of clarity that leads to this debate. To start, I would like to highlight that I am not suggesting you should build a business that is focused on something you are passionate about. I am suggesting you build a business based on purpose, and then find what you can be passionate about within that business.

This may sound the same, but it can be very different. The idea of building a business from passion is the same as the example I gave of someone that loved baking choosing to open a bakery. This is usually a bad idea.

Now if someone has a purpose to supply organic bread to the community, then they may need to open a bakery. But usually the business owner should not be the one doing the baking. Not unless he or she is a partner with someone who is passionate about the marketing and/or business systems.

The other misunderstanding about passion is that passion is something that you will love doing all the time. There may be some exceptions, but usually not.

Writers are often passionate about writing, but they will, at times, experience frustration or writer's block. Sports professionals may love their sport, but they will feel pain during extreme training, disappointment after a loss, and anger at themselves when they fail to reach a goal.

Passion is caring enough about what you do to keep doing it even when it becomes challenging or you are no longer enjoying things. It is having the desire to learn everything you can about whatever it is you are passionate about. It is having the drive to want to become the best at what you are choosing to do—no matter the pain.

A business without a purpose is almost an oxymoron. There is no reason for a business to exist without a purpose. My objective with this book is to help you realize that the purpose of your business should be greater than just making money. And whatever role you play in that business, you should be passionate about that role.

My other argument is those who argue against passion are trying to analyze the most efficient way to make money. I am fighting to find meaning and happiness in life. This is a much deeper question.

The good news is you do not need to choose one or the other. You just need more awareness of what it is you are trying to achieve and ask better questions to get you where you want to go.

To summarize… Businesses must have purpose. People must have purpose in the business they work for. People need to have passion for the work they do.

The more combined purpose and passion a business has the better its chances of success and the happier both team and customers will be.

If you cannot be passionate about starting a business, perhaps you are not an entrepreneur. There is no harm in that, as we covered early on in this book. But it is better to be honest with yourself than to be miserable trying to be something you are not.

My biggest fear is not that I would be broke (been there and done that) but that I would be financially successful at something I did not enjoy or, worse, that I was not proud of. Of course, doing something you hate and being broke is even worse. Thankfully you don't have to choose any of these options.

Create profit without compromising purpose. It may not be easy. But do what is right, not what is easy. A sense of pride, satisfaction, and accomplishment comes from overcoming challenges, not from taking the easy path.

Critics can easily find examples to prove a point. It is human nature to see what we want to see, and we want to see what supports our beliefs. If you want to change your reality, then change your beliefs, and start looking for different examples to support those new beliefs.

If you want to travel the world and take photos, then don't look for examples of people who failed; look for examples of people who succeeded. If you want to be a writer, then study the lives of successful writers.

If you want to be the founder of a business that has meaning and makes a difference in this world, then study those businesses. If you want to be a founder of a company that has passion for what they do, then immerse your focus into the story of those founders.

You will always find both naysayers and snake oil salesmen along the path. Optimists want to believe the snake oil salesmen. Pessimists will listen to the naysayers and saturate themselves in proof of failure.

Perhaps the best advice I can give you is this: You need an overwhelming, unrealistic degree of confidence in your ideas, then the determination to persist through the challenges when life shows you how unrealistically optimistic you were when you started out.

A common sentiment I hear from many successful people is "I would never have started had I known the difficulty that lay before me, but now that I have succeeded, I would never change a thing." That requires passion. And it requires a big enough purpose to give you something to believe in and be passionate about.

Through her incredible research, Professor Carol Dweck has changed the lives of thousands of children by spreading the idea of the "not yet" growth mindset. She found that some children had a brain that was literally wired for growth. Others had more of an "I can't" attitude.

Traditionally, children are rated on a pass or fail system, the only variation being how well they passed or how badly they failed. By changing the grading system to reward progress and effort more than achievement, she and her team were able to get dramatic results.

They were able to take some of the classes with the worst grades in the US, and within a year, turn them around to be amongst the best. They took children with an "I can't" attitude and changed them to an "I can; I just many not be there yet" mindset. The results speak for themselves. (To learn more, make sure you check out her TED talk.)

The problem is that most of us are conditioned from birth to believe things are black and white. That you succeeded or you did not. By adopting a more linear, growth mindset we can achieve far more.

Failure will happen before success. Don't avoid it. Deal with it.

Would you prefer to believe you can or you can't? If you keep finding reasons you can't, you won't.

So what are you waiting for? If you keep delaying things until tomorrow, you may find tomorrow passes you by or never comes.

Seize the day; go forth and prosper…

THANKS FOR READING

I hope you enjoyed the book. If so, please help share the message.

You can also help by leaving an Amazon review. Each review is very much appreciated, and helps these ideas to reach more people.

Simply follow this easy link to go direct to this books Amazon review page:

www.CreateAutomateAccelerate.com/review

Thank you.

WORKING WITH LEON

Leon works with a handful of select clients, and speaks on a select number of stages each year. If you are interested in having him help with your project then you can find out how at:

www.LeonJay.info

APPENDIX 1:
FREE RESOURCES AND TRAINING

To supplement this book we have created a resources area with links to all the books, downloadable quotes, worksheets, and expanded video commentary.

In addition to this, you can also get access to a free twenty-eight day video training program that teaches you step-by-step how to build a list to kick-start your business.

To top it off, we have also given you the link to get a free autoresponder account if you don't already have one.

To access all this additional material, simply register your copy of this book at: www.CreateAutomateAccelerate.com/access.

APPENDIX 2:
RECOMMENDED READING

The Lean Startup, by Eric Ries

20/80 Sales and Marketing, by Perry Marshall

Good to Great, by Jim Collins

Everything by Anthony Robbins

Everything by Chip and Dan Heath

Everything by Dubner and Levitt

Not mentioned, but still worth reading…

Losing My Virginity, by Richard Branson

Ca$hvertising, by Drew Eric Whitman

Predictably Irrational, by Dan Ariely

The Miracle Morning, by Hal Elrod

The Art of Thinking Clearly, by Rolf Dobelli

Leading the Starbucks Way, by Joseph Michelli

And too many others to mention here.

And don't forget…

Do Less Work, Make More Money, by Leon Jay

21 Business and Marketing Lessons from a Prostitute, by Leon Jay

APPENDIX 3: QUESTIONS FROM THROUGHOUT THIS BOOK

What is my story? What makes me who I am? What drives me? What do I really care about and stand for?

What can my business do to help or improve the lives of others?

What do I care about so much that I am willing to devote my life and my money to it in the hope of making a difference?

Why does my business exist, and what could give it even more meaning?

What do I love doing, and what am I really good at? For example, it may be team building, organizing, design, coding, marketing, or managing numbers.

What could I contribute in making my purpose a reality, be very happy doing, and find highly rewarding?

When I work as part of a team, what do I usually bring to the table?

What is the most valuable use of my time?

What tasks and responsibilities would I prefer someone else do?

Would I prefer to work with cheap labor or experts?

How and where do I find people who are committed to my purpose, passionate about what they do, highly skilled, and who will increase the quality of my team?

Where are the best people to work on my project located?

What is important to me about where I choose to live?

Where would the most advantageous place to locate my business be?

What ways are my competitors are monetizing their business?

How do other industries monetize their businesses, and what can I learn from this?

What ways can I monetize my own business and fund the achievement of my company's purpose?

Is my product the core of my business or just a way to fund a bigger purpose?

Which product or service is most appropriate for us to sell?

What am I focused on?

What is the one thing I am committed to more than anything else and am willing to sacrifice all other opportunities for to ensure I succeed?

How much money do I need to make for myself?

How much money would I like to make for myself?

How much money will the business need to generate in order to keep operating?

Do I want to be well-known or recognized as an individual? If not, am I willing to become recognized if it would be beneficial to the business?

How important is the ability for the company to run itself without me?

What is the end goal for my business?

Which is the most suitable business model to meet my objectives?

Do my business ideas so far meet all six criteria for a solid business model? If not, how can they be adjusted so that they do?

What can I do to increase the value my business delivers to its customers?

What can I do to ensure it is sustainable?

What can I do to make sure it is scalable?

What can I do to make it more profitable?

What other businesses are similar that are already proven? What can I learn from them?

What other businesses or gurus do I know of that are using this process? Exactly how are they doing it?

What elements of this four-step cycle (if any) do I already have in place?

How can I use this concept to focus my current business growth efforts?

What company brands can I think of in my industry?

What personal brands can I think of in my industry?

What would be the advantages of a company brand in fulfilling my purpose?

What would be the advantages of a personal brand in fulfilling my purpose?

How could I combine both approaches for my project, and how would that look?

What systems do I currently have in place?

What do I wish I could automate in my business the most?

Which parts of my business would benefit the most from automation?

Who makes up my current team right now?

What types of team members (partners, freelancers, employees, etc.) am I using now?

How would I benefit from working with a great team?

What could I do to be building a better team?

Which positions do I really need to start recruiting for right now?

Where would I most likely find A players for each of these positions?

What does my business look like (or will it look like) when mapped out on paper?

What are they key metrics I can identify based on my business flow?

What could I do to improve the flow of my business to make it run more optimally?

How much time have I already invested? How efficient has this been so far?

What kind of team, tools, and training does my competition have access to?

What kind of team, tools, and training do most successful companies have?

What kind of team, tools, and training do I need to get the results I want?

Which areas of this formula are my business weakest in, and what can I do about it?

What are the best- and worst-case scenarios for our growth in the next month, next three months, next six months, next year, and next three years?

In each of these scenarios and time frames, what would need to happen for that to be a reality?

Based on these answers, what are our realistic growth goals and the time frames to achieve each?

What processes do I need to put in motion today to make this happen?

What metrics do I need to measure and refine in my business?

Where do I find the data needed to measure each metric?

Who is the best person to measure and monitor the metrics for my business?

What tests can I start running today that could make a significant difference to my bottom line?

Which software is best for us to run and monitor our tests?

Do I need to find someone else to run the testing for me? If so, who?

Which ways can we reduce our operational costs without affecting quality?

Which ways could we generate more customers?

How can we increase the average amount customers spend with each transaction?

Which ways could we get customers to buy again?

What are my customers saying? What are they asking for? What can I learn from this?

What areas of my business can benefit most from applying the 64/4 principle?

Which of my tasks today are 64/4 principle tasks?

How can I teach this concept to my entire team to improve their effectiveness?

What can I let go of in my daily routine that is not serving any real purpose?

How can I find more time to focus on what really matters?

Which strategies am I going to adopt to increase my efficiency?

What are my current excuses for not achieving the success or results I want?

What can I do to overcome these excuses?

How can I teach others in my company to do the same?

ABOUT THE AUTHOR

Leon Jay is an international author and seminar speaker on the topic of online business. He has spoken in the UK, NZ, Australia, America, Thailand, Vietnam, Singapore, China, Indonesia, and Israel.

He started out building a web development business, which he passed on to a business partner, so he could pursue the world of affiliate and information marketing.

Since then, he has served as an affiliate manager for a seven-figure-a-year Australian personal development company and as Director of Marketing for Mark Joyner Inc. (Mark is known as the Godfather of Internet marketing and is credited as being the first person to have sold an e-book).

Leon has also been the marketing mind and 50 percent partner in a software and training program launch that generated $1.4 million in ten days. He has consulted and partnered on various other six- and seven -figure launches, is founder of www.FusionHQ.com (a platform for digital and information markers) and www.send.fish (an autoresponder service), co-founded www.CopySniper.com (an online copywriting software and sales page builder), and is co-founder of Coffee Monster (a cafe and co-working space for digital nomads in Chiang Mai, Thailand).

In 2012, he was featured on the cover of *Internet Marketing Magazine*, a space reserved only for those who have generated more than seven figures online. He has also been featured in several books, as well as having been invited to be a guest speaker on many podcast shows and webinars.

His industry expertise is highly valued. Clients have paid $10,000 a day for private coaching with him.

In addition to all this, he has hosted multiple live events and webinars of his own to help share his knowledge and enthusiasm for building businesses online.

His books are no fluff and contain a fresh, direct, and often controversial take on the subject matter. He has little patience for nonsense, fads, or parroting other people's content.

www.ingramcontent.com/pod-product-compliance
Lightning Source LLC
Chambersburg PA
CBHW070852180526
45168CB00005B/1793